THE INDIA CENTURY
VISION 2047

Economy, Security,
Geopolitics and Beyond

THE INDIA CENTURY
VISION 2047

Economy, Security,
Geopolitics and Beyond

Ashok Pathak

BHARAT GLOBAL INDUSTRIES FORUM

PENTAGON PRESS LLP

First published in 2025 by

PENTAGON PRESS LLP
206, Peacock Lane, Shahpur Jat
New Delhi-110049, India
Contact: 011-26490600

Typeset in Century Schoolbook, 11 Point
Printed at Aegean Offset Printers, Greater Noida

ISBN 978-81-991162-3-8

www.pentagonpress.in

Contents

संदेश

स्वदेशी जागरण मंच के तत्वावधान में शुरू किया गया भारत वैश्विक उद्योग मंच, भारत को विश्व का विनिर्माण केंद्र बनाने के लिए समर्पित है। यह उच्चतम गुणवत्ता की अवधारणा से प्रेरित होकर, वैश्विक बाजारों के लिए एक वैकल्पिक आपूर्ति श्रृंखला विकल्प प्रदान करेगा और निश्चित ही भारत को समृद्ध और सशक्त बनाएगा।

ब्रिगेडियर (डॉ.) अशोक पाठक द्वारा लिखित 'द इंडिया सेंचुरी विज़न 2047: इकोनॉमी, सिक्योरिटी, जियोपॉलिटिक्स एंड बियॉन्ड', तथ्य-आधारित और वस्तुनिष्ठ तो है ही साथ ही कोरोना जैसी वैश्विक महामारी के समय भारत की नवोन्मेषिता व भारत की "वसुधैव कुटुंबकम्" की भावना को पुस्तक में अच्छी तरह प्रदर्शित किया गया है।

यह पुस्तक उद्योग से जुड़े विभिन्न विषयों के लिए प्रेरक बनकर भारत को आर्थिक दृष्टि से सशक्त बनाने में निश्चत ही सहायक सिद्ध होगी।

रामलाल
अखिल भारतीय संपर्क प्रमुख
आरएसएस

Foreword

India had been an economic growth engine for the world and global military power for thousand of years till as late as beginning of seventeenth century – not a distant past in the life of nations. Today we are at the cusp of moving from a developing to a developed nation tag. This would need major transformation in the character of our society and industry.

Our industries need to be more inclined to contribute to the society and the citizens. We need to focus on creation of new knowledge and technology rather than just using technologies given to us by the West. Our entrepreneurs need to be self motivated and committed to create wealth for the nation rather than seek government help and subsidies. The creation of Bharat Global Industries Forum under the aegis of Swadeshi Jagran Manch will serve to achieve these broad objectives,

The Indian youth are known for their IT skills world over. This needs to be harnessed with the help of AI and quantum computing to achieve higher quality of manufacturing at lower costs. In our journey to a developed nation, we need to remember that the strategic model that we follow needs to be based on the vast experience and knowledge base we have as the most ancient civilization on the planet. Our philosophy is oneness of humanity and one planet for all living and non living. Thus, ***ekatmvad*** is the mantra we need to follow. My growth can not be at the cost of your loss. No zero-sum game in our economic policies.

India today is not a follower we are vying for global leadership in economy, international security and geopolitics. I found Brig (Dr) Ashok Pathak's fact based and easy to understand analysis of challenges and silver lining in realizing our vision of developed nation by 2047 very realistic and stimulating intellectual discourse. I am sure that readers belonging to all sections will enjoy going through the contents.

Satish Kumar
Sah Sangthak
Swadeshi Jagran Manch

Preface

At midnight 15 August 1947, the Tricolor flew over the Indian skies. Most of the British left leaving the last Viceroy – Lord Mountbatten to guide a free nation to train its leadership how to govern! The British Military top brass continued to lead the Indian services till the Indian military commanders learnt how to handle a military force! The Indian Prime Minister continued to seek advice from the British Parliament on critical issues such as Tibet, fighting a war with Pakistan and so on. The West – first the British, then the US served as a beacon for growth. Did the Englishmen deserve this?

Shashi Tharoor found the British the worst plunderers of India's wealth – looting some US $ 45 trillion in their rule stretching three centuries. M J Akbar noticed that a record 34 famines occurred in India – some of these were 'British made' that killed Indians in billions. Post 1947 India grew at a rate of two to three percent. It was worse than the lowest in the world (that included the sub-Saharan region). This continued for next three decades till 1976. Then the growth picked up to around four percent. Thanks to the International Monetary Fund (IMF) in 1991 the economy was unshackled. But the mindset remained the same.

Meanwhile in 1949 India lost one-third of Jammu and Kashmir to Pakistan in a war that India was winning. In 1959 China held on to some 38000 square kms of Indian territory in Aksai Chin. Post 1990 the insurgency in the J&K took a heavy toll on men and material for the next three decades.

On 18 May 2014, *The Guardian* of UK observed in its editorial that '18 May 2014 will go down in history when the British finally left India'. Hence when we analyze 'Viksit Bharat Vision 2047', this background needs to be taken into account. The historical baggage that has formed a collective self-image comprises three distinct periods, each adding to the learning curve. Post 2014 a transformational process was set in motion that created its own currents and headwinds since the people were not used to reforms at such a fast pace. Ironically the national self-belief took a massive leap of faith during the worst period of COVID-19. Post COVID India surprised the world with its unexpected resilience and growth. Since then, the nation has not looked back. Though the journey to Vision 2047 is seemingly audacious, the silver linings seen during the past five years and the Prime Minister's speech delivered on 15 August 2025 are reassuring. The Prime Minister's speech in fact laid down a broad road-map for realising the vision that the NITI Aayog has set for 2047. Considering the significance of the Prime Minister's speech, the highlights as given by the Government are included as an Appendix. Three issues that the Prime Minister covered in his speech briefly are most relevant to us. Hence these are analyzed in greater detail in the Appendix. These are economic self-reliance/ resilience, security and new normal for India's geopolitical world order.

We have three issues to address for analyzing the possibility of Vision 2047 meeting all its goals. First the outlines of historical baggage, finer aspects of Vision 2047 and silver linings that can form the stepping stone for accelerated growth. The second part addresses the economy, followed by military power. Finally, geopolitics that is powered by economic and military strength.

For the ideas for Viksit Bharat 2047 to get implemented in right earnest someone and some organisations need to dedicate their personal and organisational energies at grass root levels – with the people, industries and the administration for converting ideas into reality. It is here that Shri Satish Kumar from the Sah Sangthak Swadeshi Jagran Manch has very selflessly committed himself and the organisation to make the lofty goals a reality. He persuaded the big industrial units to form the Bharat Global Industries Forum (BGIF) and is spearheading the movement to create the right ecosystem that can jettison the baggage of the colonial past and place India on the Kautilyan trajectory that synergises economy, military power to gain and sustain a leadership role in global geopolitics.

It had been some time while I was collecting ideas and data for this book. This preparation was brought to conclusion when I met Rajan Arya of Pentagon Press LLP. His commitment, enthusiasm and professional skills were contagious. The book finally took shape in record time due to determined efforts of Team Pentagon Press.

Ashok Pathak

Chapter One

Introduction

Challenges of Overcoming Monumental Inertia

The ease or degree of difficulty in completing the journey towards the goals can be gauged by the internal and external environment shaped by two factors. How did India behave so far and how international contours changed over time. This will help the national leadership and people at large to plan their journey towards a developed India.

The post World War II period from 1945 to 1960, saw countries becoming independent or attaining 'self-governed' status. India was one of these with some unique distinctions. First it was one of the very few decolonised countries in 1947 that were partitioned. Second even after being declared an independent country India opted to retain a British military commander as their first Governor General – Lord Mountbatten, who retained this position for about ten months (15 August 1947 to June 1948). Third, British officers were retained to head the Indian Armed Forces on the premise that since the 'native' Indian officers in the army have no experience of functioning at high ranks they would need a few years of handholding. A British officer headed the Corps of Signals of the Indian Army till 1954. Fourth, for all strategic decisions pertaining to nation building British advice was sought and followed.

What did the British do to deserve this honour? In 1600 India's GDP at the prevailing international dollar rates was $ 74,250 million and the British GDP was $ 6,700 million. When the British left, India's GDP was $ 2,55,852 million and that of Britain $ 3,14,969 million. A total of 34 major famines occurred during a time window of 120 years during British rule. This was double the number of famines which India faced in 2000 years preceding British rule. From 1765 to 1938 Britain drained $45 trillion from India – 17 times the current GDP of the UK. Shashi Tharoor (*An Era of Darkness*) quotes British MP Dr Rutherford, 'In return for India's invaluable service during the war (World War I) we gave to the Indian nation such a discreditable, disgraceful and tyrannical constitution.' So what explains the propensity to follow the footsteps of such a colonial master? Inheritance of legacy of inertia. Monumental resistance to change. There are three major factors that explain the monumental inertia. First the complex nature of India's 'freedom struggle' and the texture of India's indigenous political leadership that took over from the British colonisers. Second the internal strife in India with a number of subnational undercurrents. Third an unrealistic and ill-informed geopolitical visualisation by the Indian leadership in 1947.

In terms of economic growth and resilience most economists divide India's growth story since independence into three phases. The first phase from 1950 to 1980 is generally termed as wasted years. Between 1950 and 1980, India's growth rate averaged around 3.5 percent per annum and this was at a time when the developing world, including Sub-Saharan Africa and other least-developed countries, showed a growth rate of 5.2 percent per annum. Then came the second phase from 1980 to 1990 where the growth picked up accompanied by profligate spending leading to economic disaster. In 1980, first attempts were made to open up the economy and also embrace Information Technology (IT). The GDP growth rate jumped to 5.6 percent, which by Indian standards was good though the world around us was growing at a much faster pace. However, during this period, government spending was profligate and a large-scale revenue deficit was created. Besides the public sector became more inefficient. This was a time when India went to IMF to save herself from defaulting on foreign debt payment. IMF did help but triggered liberalisation of India's economy. It was a very fortunate intervention for the Indian economy. The third phase from 1991 to 2014 is the period post liberalisation. The Indian economy started growing at 6 to 7 percent. By 2004-05 the growth rate was almost close to 8 and 9 percent. The period of 2009 to 2014 was marked by high interest rates, stagnating high deficit, weak currency, loss of accountability and highest levels of scams unprecedented in the history of India's independence. Some economists and political scientists call this period the lost decade.

India became a free nation in the wake of communal divide that created Pakistan. Also the Indian political leadership was under strong influence of communist China and Soviet Russia. This placed Indian people in the cauldron of subnational/communally charged movements and Left-wing propaganda. Both these aspects ensured politics with a communal flavour and misplaced pursuit of socialism. Consequently, for the next 24 years India became poorer and produced more illiterate people. Not taking a decision, stalling good decisions, extending State control over almost all citizen activities and getting accustomed to near stagnation became a dominant culture. Above all, the Indian political leadership and consequently a huge section of the intelligentsia viewed nationalism, nationalistic ideology and patriotism through the prism of the erstwhile colonial masters or through communist concepts.

Hence when we analyse the factors that are likely to help or obstruct the path to achieving Vision 2047 the historical baggage cannot be ignored, because the people, leaders and the ecosystem would be affected by these very factors.

Vision 2047

The NITI Aayog Paper on Vision 2047 envisages Indian GDP in 2047 touching $ 30 trillion, along with a per capita of $ 18000. This would translate into about an eight-fold rise in GDP and nine-fold rise in GDP per capita. Annual economic growth will have to be maintained between 7 and 8 percent. The key areas for the government in this journey range from green energy hubs, water security and optimising urban delivery of public service, universal basic income, fast paced industrial development, and making India a global hub for manufacturing. Incidentally as late as in October 2024, the government figures on contribution of manufacturing to the GDP was just 14 percent, agriculture contributed 17.66 percent. For more than half the population agriculture is the main occupation (54.6 percent). Increasing the per capita GDP is a serious challenge.

How does the NITI Aayog look at the ecosystem? To start with the Aayog accepts the fact that comparable countries (especially China) were at the same level as India in the 1960s and 1970s. We have seen in the earlier section how India languished at the bottom for more than five decades. During this period China and other countries like Germany, the US and Japan made phenomenal progress. Hence it becomes necessary to analyse what these countries did to forge ahead. Second – a very pertinent issue is, 'equality based on personal motivation and capability'. This translates into the role of the government to create a 'nationwide Tsunami of development' through transformation to rise to the envisaged levels. It is not just the GDP or the per capita in the set of goals. Here are some more daunting objectives to be achieved:

- World class social services to 1.6 billion population (assuming that this would be the population in 2047).
- Create interfaces for learning, governance and health care – e-learning, e-governance and tele-medicine.
- Create AI based expert systems for governance – e-Kautilya, e-Chanakya, e-Manu.
- Massive IT infrastructure for education – (e-Acharya), Skilling (e-Guru) and health (e-Vaid).

Given the existing level of ICT penetration in India, digital infrastructure, even if created, will not be of much use due to lack of commensurate skills and availability of resources with the people. Hence the hybrid – physical and digital (phygital) will have to be adopted with gradual shift to completely digital.

The government has very rightly envisaged that for reaching the desired levels of GDP and distribution of wealth India needs to become a manufacturing hub. At present we are nowhere in this race. China started the journey more than two-and-a-half decades back. By 2022 it reached a stage where it captured one-fifth of the global market for manufactured exports. This happened at the cost of the US, Germany and Japan. From 2000 to 2025 China jumped from around 3.5 percent of the global share to almost 20 percent, whereas the US declined from 13.5 percent to around 6 percent, Germany from 9.5 percent to 7.5 percent and Japan from 9.5 percent to 3.5 percent. China took two major initiatives. First it started welcoming global companies (primarily of the US) to manufacture in China. Second it created a Communist Party-driven campaign for a Export-led Import Substituting Infrastructure Driven (ELISID) Plan. China always aspired to achieve an economy of scale. Hence there is nothing like micro, small and medium-scale industries.

Arvind Virmani's Paper of July 2024 analyses the national and international security matrix as power pyramid and geopolitics. As regards the power pyramid the economy occupies the base segment that supports the military and diplomacy. Interestingly both economy and military are driven by technology. While general technology drives the economy, strategic technology drives military power. Even geopolitics is driven by global economy and the international security environment.

If we look at what Vision 2047 envisages, where the global leaders like China and the US and in terms of the economy Germany and Japan are today, and what has been India's journey so far, the task looks daunting – almost impossible. But there are some silver linings created during the last decade. It is a matter of how we the people of India accelerate so that the giant fly wheel of growth gains enough momentum. Let us look at the silver linings – something that validates, *The Guardian's* observation that the 'Britishers finally left India on 18 May 2014'!

Some Silver Linings

During the past decade India has achieved lofty goals that were beyond imagination of the generation that followed the West. All these landmark achievements came against strong headwinds. When the world was reeling under one of the most devastating pandemics, everyone who mattered expected the Indian economy to be decimated and Indian citizens to suffer the worst. No one expected India to develop its own vaccine. Post COVID-19 India not only proved the *naysayers* wrong, but vaccinated Indian citizens with two billion dozes (two dozes per citizen in most cases). Besides, 101 countries were provided Indian COVID-19 vaccines. These included developed nations such as Canada, Australia, the UK, and the Netherlands. Several least developed nations were provided vaccines for free. Besides India also helped countries with the supply of 1.8 million tons of wheat. These included countries like Switzerland, Israel, Qatar, Yemen, Bangladesh and Sri Lanka. Afghanistan was gifted 3,80,000 MT of wheat as aid against 50,000 MT earmarked for them. Thus, India emerged as main player in the global food security plan.

Post-COVID India emerged as a leading economy in the world – a position that continues till date. The IMF on 12 November 2021 projected India's growth at 9.5 percent in 2022 and 8.5 percent in the next fiscal. Both these are highest growth rates in the world. India had fourteen start-up unicorns in the top one thousand such start-ups in the world in 2021, ahead of developed countries such as Japan, South Korea and Israel. There are 150 Indian companies that are propelling national economic growth. The fastest growing companies in this group came up in 2014 (two) and 2015 (seven). Many of the companies in this group are innovation-driven technology enterprises. The growth rate of companies that came up in 2014 and 2015, ranges from 77 percent to 4449 percent.

During the period 2014 to 2021 the per day average of highway construction rose to 25 kilometres, three times more than the previous regime. In 2021 the average length of highways constructed per day jumped to 36.4 kilometres. In rural India roads measuring 2.33 lakh kilometres were constructed during the last seven years.

India's performance in adopting digital economy has been remarkable by any standards. Even the Indian parliamentarians did not expect India to adopt this clean and transparent system of financial transactions. However the recent PwC Report accepts India as a global leader in digital transactions. They forecast that other nations in the world – including the developed one, would follow the Indian Unified Payments Interface (UPI) system.

In the semiconductor sector, though India started very late, the volume of investments, creation of competitive environment, public-private participation, foreign collaboration, involvement of academia and the pace at which production and innovation are taking. This is very encouraging. There are six partnerships in the field. Big IT majors like HCL, Tata Electronics, Tata Semiconductor Manufacturing, Murugappa Group, CG, among others, are in the field. Foxconn of Taiwan, Japanese and South Korean semiconductor manufacturing firms are working in collaboration with Indian companies. The Malaysian government – encouraged by India's rapid progress in the field, has shown interest in partnering with India. More than seven hundred universities and best engineering colleges are creating high quality human capital in the field of design and development. One of the universities has produced wafers ready for production line. A team from the

Indian Institute of Science (IISC) have made the biggest breakthrough by submitting a Report for producing 2D chips that would have thickness much less than the three nanometers thickness for which only Taiwan had the expertise. The chip developed by the IISC Bengaluru will be in Angstrom – ten times thinner than a nanometer. This would revolutionise the computing and ICT industries. The iPhones of tomorrow may be powered by Indian chips – so would be the new generation weapon systems – cyber security, cyber attack, RADARS, satellites, avionics for the aircraft, even AI-enabled fighter aircraft engines, automobiles and all appliances/equipment that need Supervisory Control and Data Acquisition (SCADA) capabilities.

Another area where India has broken the glass sealing is space. During the last ten years ISRO has launched 394 satellites; these include satellites of 34 countries – 232 satellites of the US, 83 of the UK and 9 of Singapore. On 15 February 2017, ISRO launched 104 satellites from one rocket – a world record. The space sector has since been corporatised with major involvement of the private sector. At present 52 satellites are being developed for surveillance and perhaps target acquisition and guidance systems. Of these 21 are being developed by ISRO and 31 by the private sector. Space has emerged as an area of military dominance, research, and digital infrastructure.

Indigenisation of defence production has been another area where India has shown remarkable growth. From a net importer India has emerged as a net exporter. The government has ambitious goals of surpassing ₹ 35,000 crore worth of defence exports. The grand success of Operation SINDOOR has given another boost to the Indian exports in the defence sector.

During the planning and conduct of Operation SINDOOR, India jumped many notches higher in geopolitical projection. The political leadership did not waste time in 'creating international support' for taking decisions on national security. India declared zero tolerance for terrorism and advised the world to adopt the same policy against terrorism.

India declared no 'holds barred' threat if the adversary persists with nefarious activities against India. The Indus Water Treaty (IWT) that was considered sacrosanct no matter how many Indian citizens Pakistan based terrorists kill or irrespective of unprovoked attacks on India, was held in abeyance.

On the military front, 36 ships – led by the aircraft carrier *INS Vikrant*, breathed down the Pakistani port of Karachi by conducting naval exercises that included live firing of missiles. On 6 and 7 May 2025, one of the most daring and precise attacks deep inside Pakistan on Markaz Subhan Allah in Bahawalpur, Markaz Taiba in Muridke Lahore, Sarjal and Mehmoona Joya in Sialkot and five camps in the Pakistan-Occupied Jammu and Kashmir (POJK) – Barnala in Bhimber, Abbas Kotli and Gurpur in Kotli, Sawai Nala and Syedna Bilal in Muzaffarabad were conducted. When Pakistan launched counter attacks, India targeted Pakistani military installations from Skardu in the North (POJK) to Bholari in the South. Military airbases at Noorkhan, Rafiqui, Murid, Chaklala, Sukkur, Sialkot, Pasrur, Chunian, Sargodha, Skardu, Bholari, Jacobabad and Rahimyarkhan were destroyed. As per the international experts on air warfare (Tom Cooper of Austria) the Pakistani nuclear site near Kirana Hills and Sargodha were hit by the Indian strikes. This as per several experts made the Pakistani nukes unusable. However, the Indian official statement denies such a claim.

The Indian armed forces took just 88 hours to bring the Pakistan armed forces on their knees. But something more unexpected happened. The Indian strikes made both the US and China wary of Indian military strength and audacity. The US leadership who were declaring a strategic partnership suddenly did a volte face and came in support of Pakistan. Thus the cover on the deception was blown. India and the world learnt that all the talk of richest and largest democracies coming together was a farce. The US and Britain have always treated Pakistan as their vassal State. Besides, the narrative of Chinese arms supremacy took a beating. Both these factors will impose tremendous resistance to India's march towards Vision 2047.

With this introduction the discussion is now primed to address the three major aspects of Vision 2047 – the economy, military power and geopolitics.

Chapter Two

Economy

In Search of a Model

We have two options in benchmarking. First look at how other countries have done this – say China the US and even Germany and Japan. Another way to do this is compare India of the present with Bharat of the past.

We need to be very clear that any country will adopt a course of action or strategy based on four fundamental factors. First, what that country thinks of itself that defines its self-image. A non-negotiable value system and desired position in the global order. Second, the leadership matrix or more directly the political system the nation has. Third, the resources it has and finally, the international support or resistance the country faces to realise the vision.

China's Journey from a Third World Country in 1950 to a Super Power in 2025

China's history as a nation dates back to 4000 years (1700 BC). Henry Kissinger in his book, *World Order* describes the Chinese vision – driven by their 'middle kingdom' self-belief whereby the Chinese Emperor (now ruling party) has a divine sanction to rule the world. This self-concept makes them believe that they are the only civilised people on the planet; all other civilisations are barbarian. Even the heads of state of other sovereign nations are expected to pay obeisance to the Emperor. The tradition to kowtow (kneeling before the Emperor) was expected from other heads of state, since China considered other states as tributary States (*China and the World Order*, p. 221)

Mao Zedong proclaimed that power flows from the barrel of the gun. Between 1951 to 1979 China fought wars with the US in Korea in 1951, with India in 1962, with Russia in 1963, and with Vietnam in 1979. It has border disputes with more than 16 countries. The urge to dominate other nations in all fields has been the Chinese trait since 1949. To reach the top in every field, China has been able to reinvent herself at least thrice during the past seven decades.

On the economic front the first two decades since 1949 have not been very fruitful. Especially, the period of the Great Leap Forward under Mao was a disaster. It was in 1970 that China commenced liberalisation of her economy. In 1979 it formalised trade relations with the US. Post 1980 China embarked upon rapid economic growth. It was the US that helped China grow economically. This was also the time that China liberalised the economy, welcomed multinational companies to establish production and service centres in China (on Chinese terms), learnt free market systems of management, invested heavily in infrastructure, technology absorption, research and development, education. By 2012 China was the second largest economy after the US – overtaking Germany. They have not looked back. By 2025 they have overtaken almost every country in terms of Purchasing Power Parity and share of exports of manufactured goods. In nominal terms they are behind the US with a US $ 17 trillion GDP and a per capita of more than US $ 12000.

The Chinese leadership commenced their journey for this spectacular growth with a goal to be the best in the world – in terms of economic strength, knowledge, production and military power. China started with a literacy rate of 47.5 percent in 1950 and achieved 94.5 percent by 2020. India reached a literacy rate of 62.6 percent during this period. China has twelve universities in the top hundred in the world. None of the Indian universities were ranked in this bracket. Chinese universities spend US $ 25,692 million on research per year; eight times more compared to US $ 3,255 million spent by the Indian educational institutions annually. A whopping 34 percent of all international students studying in the US were Chinese (2020) compared to 18 percent Indian students. China spent two percent of its GDP on research and development in 2020 against 0.7 percent by India. While the Indian government spent US $ 29,185 million on research and development, the Chinese government spent US $ 58,838 million during that period. Chinese business enterprises (industries) spent US $ 2,87,795.3 million on research compared to just US $ 19,214 million by Indian industries. China has 1,089 researchers per million students against just 156 researchers per million in India.

As on 12 June 2025 China had fifteen companies amongst the top hundred Forbes' 2000 list. India had just four in this category. However when it comes to the best companies in terms of investment on their workforce none of the Chinese or the Indian companies figure in this list. It may be interesting to see the level of Chinese domination in manufacturing. China ranks first in the manufacturing of steel with more than 1200 million tons of steel per year, followed by India, ranked second. India produced 149 million tons of steel in the same year. China's shipbuilding order book in 2024 was for 1700 ships. The US produced less than ten ships that year. The Chinese shipbuilding industry has 70 percent of global orders for building new ships. Similarly China controls the Lithium Ion battery market for the electric vehicles and other appliances, and manufacturing of solar panels. They also dominate the rare earth mineral holdings and processing market. The list is long and it has become quite difficult for even the US to compete with China in manufacturing. The Chinese journey to these dizzy heights was based on the following factors:

- Tight command and control by a single political party.
- Capability to change course when the situation demanded.
- Thinking big, no room for small industries, entrepreneurship.
- Geopolitical dominance and hence huge investment in defence.
- Exploit economic power to capture foreign markets and influence their politics.
- Massive investment in R&D and creating economy of scale.
- During the first three decades China focused on skills development so that a strong base can be built for manufacturing – moving the population from agrarian economy to manufacturing work in the factories.
- Post-1979, opened up the education system for global competition.

The US

In Henry Kissinger's words no country other than the US has played such a decisive role in shaping contemporary world order. The US has proclaimed itself as a nation that would shape the destiny of mankind. As per the Americans their principles are universal and any country not following these are living in some kind of unsatisfactory, probationary arrangement. What is more dangerous is the fact the US has not hesitated to change or subvert governments of other nations through non-military and military means. What we see today in international dynamics is that the US has arrogated for itself the role of the global police. It is the US that decides on economic sanctions against a nation by all other countries in the world. Thus while imposing sanctions on Iran the US ordains all other nations to do the same, ditto with Russia. They took an astonishing decision to freeze all Russian foreign exchange reserves in international banks. The US wants all countries to trade in US dollars. Any country that violates this is threatened with heavy tariffs or worse.

The US has backed this self-imposed world leader belief with some monumental achievements. More than half of top 100, Forbes 2000 companies are of US origin. Amongst the top 100 best companies in the world again US companies number more than half. In terms of market cap among the top ten, eight companies are American (one company each of Saudi Arabia and Taiwan in this bracket). Among the top fifty companies in terms of market capitalisation there are thirty-three US and just six Chinese companies. The top Indian company in this category is Reliance Industries ranked at 54th position, India's HDFC Bank is ranked at 79.

What makes the American companies excel globally? While Jim Collins would like us to believe in factors like leadership, vision, culture and so on that have made the best performing American companies do such an outstanding job, the ground realities are different. When the US entered World War II it had no military experience of fighting a modern war, that the other Allied and Axis powers had. But America had companies that could produce goods – including war material. These companies went into full swing to keep the Allied forces equipped and moving. After the War the Americans emerged as the factory of the world. True to American culture, almost all these companies were private enterprises.

Just after the War the US designed and managed the global economy in a way that served its economic and strategic interests. Launching the Marshall Plan for recovery of Germany in particular and Europe in general, rebuilding Japan under Field Marshal McArthur, routing the oil economy of the Middle East through American dollars – all these factors ensured that the US remained the most prosperous nation, militarily the strongest and also the most attractive nation for people to do business, acquire knowledge, conduct research and lead a life of freedom and prosperity. The strategic approach followed by the US were based on the following:

Military might, economic and geopolitical goals synergised. The US spends 62.3 percent of all the defence expenditure in the world. China (18.6 percent) and Russia (8.8 percent) spend not even half of what the Americans do. We note that Russia spends an insignificantly small amount compared to the US on defence though it has been engaged in a war with Ukraine for more than three years. After the attack on Pearl Harbour by the Japanese no nation has attacked the US mainland. Even then the US forces have fought in Korea, Vietnam, Iraq and Afghanistan. They lost more than one lakh American soldiers in these wars. The US has five regional theatre commands (total nine commands). Except one of these, four other regional commands operate outside the US. The US African Command is to strengthen defence capabilities of African nations. The Central Command is responsible for cooperation among the nations in the Middle East and increase regional stability. The European Command works in tandem with the NATO nations for security and defence of Europe, some nations of the Middle East and Eurasia. The Indo-Pacific Command enhances development and regional security in conjunction with the partner nations. The Northern Command is the only US Theatre Command that is responsible for security of the US, primarily homeland security. The Southern Command is responsible for South American nations.

Audacious goals to dominate global economy and power Matrix. Several US multinational companies have global footprints with market capitalisation in trillions of dollars. The NVDIA market cap is US $ 4 trillion. The supply chain of these companies are spread across the globe.

Attracted the best talent from across the globe. The US has not only invested heavily in higher education and research, they created an ecosystem that attracts the best in the world. Almost one-third of the international students studying in the US are from China – their fierce global competitor.

Education for creating more entrepreneurs. The US higher education system does not train job seekers, instead they emphasise on job creators.

Close links between the academia and industry. Most of their universities have sizeable campuses allotted to industry houses. Hence the academia and industry have close links.

Generated and sustained an environment of creating, exploiting new technologies through research and innovation. Almost all new technologies emanate from the US R&D centres and academia.

What Model should India Follow?

It is very tempting to suggest that India must follow the Chinese model because we started almost at the same time (August 1947 for India and October 1949 for China). Also we have some parity in population. On the other hand, the US model also looks tempting to emulate because both are democracies. A very realistic answer to this is that size, population or the form of government do not make nations similar. In the case of China the similarities end with population and with the US, democratic government is the only similarity. We will be able to understand our stark differences by looking at the challenges of India's macro-economic ecosystem.

India: Challenges of Macro-economic Ecosystem

We will first discuss the challenges as seen from the prism of modern economic theory and then in the light of Indian philosophy of oneness *(ekatmata)*. The Indian Finance Minister Ms Sitharaman is quoted in *The Hindu* that the top 22 percent of Indian companies with a turnover of over ₹ 50 crores per year contribute 90 percent to GST collection, while only two percent of individuals in India pay income tax and half of all companies in India pay zero tax. Again, 90 percent of the companies earn just ₹ 50 lakhs per year. A whopping 84 percent of the companies pay nothing in an overall contribution of ₹ 7.16 lakh crores in a year.

Ananth Nageshwaran (*Perspective Political Economic Approach,* VIF, New Delhi) commented that the Indian macro economic structural framework has a marked anti big bias. Non-agricultural unincorporated enterprises contributed ₹ 11.5 trillion. In contrast less than two lakh (0.2 million) contributed ₹ 11.6 trillion in the same year. Just 4.1 percent of Indian corporates have more than 500 employees that contribute 60 percent of the GVA. The share of around 63 million MSMEs to the GDP has remained around 30 percent of the GDP. In fact, during most of the years this contribution was even below 30 percent while the number of MSMEs remained more or less the same. The remaining 70 percent comes from the formal corporate organisations. Thus, things have not changed much. Besides, 45 percent of the exports are from the MSMEs while the rest are from the corporates. What are the reasons behind this lopsided productivity? A NITI Aayog survey in 2017 found that firms with 100 and more employees took longer to get approvals, faced more regulatory obstacles and paid higher costs of compliance. The government gives several incentives to corporate enterprises – like national manufacturing competitiveness, government presence and price preference policies, credit-linked capital subsidy, credit guarantee fund scheme, MSME cluster development programme, quality upgradation, micro finance. All the financial and regulatory incentives are reserved for the micro, small and medium enterprises. No incentive for large enterprises (except of course the Production Linked Incentives). One of the reasons for this is the social and political perception about the wealth creators. The owner of a big corporate house is considered to be a crook by the people and of course the politicians. The politicians see the rich as convenient cash cows for availing donation and then flog them in their political narrative. China encourages companies to achieve economy of massive scales. The US celebrates the achievements of the corporate entities as they grow rich.

However it must be admitted that as far as the government policies are concerned there has been a major shift in encouraging corporate organisations to grow rich and big. India levies 30 percent corporate tax – most countries are around this mark – China levies 25 percent, the US federal Corporate Income Tax (CIT) is 25 percent but their state taxation is as low as one to two percent. In UK it is 25 percent. A point of caution here. Organisations do not grow or improve based on external stimuli (government incentives), the internal dynamics such as their culture and leadership are the major contributors in their road to excellence.

Interestingly when it comes to the top thirty richest persons in the world, India equals China. Two persons from India and three from China are on that list. Of course most of these thirty people are from the US. Incidentally the richest person in India is richer than the richest person in China. When it comes to the richest companies China is miles ahead of India. This is an interesting pointer to the societal dynamics in India.

If we go by the Boston Consulting Group (BCG) matrix in business strategies, the bulk of the Indian businesses are happy profiteering from the cash cow. Thus there is a clear intention of making quick and maximum profit. There is no effort to invest in research and development to capitalise from the star section that requires investment in R&D, involves risk factor but also gives an opportunity to make heavy profit when the research starts delivering. As per Government of India, just half the corporate entities make any investment in R&D; similarly just 36 of the 70-

odd public sector companies make any investment in R&D. Here also, it is the defence sector where investment in R&D as percentage of turnover is the highest and has grown year on year since 2022. The next three are pharma, automobile and health care. The remaining sectors spend less than two percent of their turnover on R&D. Though a large majority of corporate entities spend nothing on R&D, they also do not contribute to the GST and remain happy being in the zero tax bracket!!

Globally, leading corporate leadership and think tanks confirm that this is the age of technology and knowledge. Among the top 50 Indian companies by market cap, just six are technology companies (TCS, Infosys, L&T, Sun Pharma, HAL and BEL). Of these Hindustan Aeronautics Limited (HAL) and Bharat Electronics Limited (BEL) are public sector companies and are primarily involved in defence production. Similarly Larsen and Toubro (L&T) is also participating in defence production. None of these are amongst the global leaders. In China among the top 50 Chinese companies eight are technology companies – and these companies are way ahead of Indian technology companies in market cap, investment in R&D and efficiency. India is doing very well in the number of start-ups. But here again India's Commerce Minister Mr Piyush Goyal was anguished to say that start-ups are inclined towards lucrative profitable zones and are not scaling up.

In the US and China the academics-industry synergy drives growth. The US universities claim that they do not prepare their students for jobs, instead they prepare job creators. Most of the premier US universities and higher education institutes have almost half the campus allotted to corporate houses. In China the government invests heavily into higher education – China has several universities among the top 100 globally. In our case a *Times of India* Report states that 'more you learn less you earn'. More than half of Indian graduates are unemployable. The Government of India has brought in the New Educational Policy in 2020. Hopefully the impact of this policy will be seen in times to come. Another aspect that gets ignored in this unemployment data is what are the business entities doing in creating and acquiring talent as also retaining it? A case study of performance and dedication of Taj Hotel staff during the 26/11 terrorist attack will be very relevant here.

Talent Hunt, Transformation and Retention 'The Taj' Way

About 35 Taj Mumbai employees, led by a 24-year-old banquet manager, Mallika Jagad, were assigned to manage the event in a second-floor banquet room. During the onslaught on Taj Mumbai, 31 people died and 28 were injured. Its guests were overwhelmed by employees' dedication to duty, their desire to protect guests without regard to personal safety, and their quick thinking. Restaurant and banquet staff rushed people to safe locations such as kitchens and basements. Telephone operators stayed at their posts, alerting guests to lock doors and not step out. Kitchen staff formed human shields to protect guests during evacuation attempts. As many as 11 Taj Mumbai employees laid down their lives while helping between 1,200 and 1,500 guests escape.

How and from where did the Taj Hotel find this talent? What did they look for in these young women and men when they picked them up for the job? How did they train and retain them? These are the questions that every business entity that is struggling to get and retain talent must analyse.

- Pick them up fresh. They always sought fresh recruits rather than lateral hires.
- Adopt a values – driven recruitment system such as respect for elders and teachers, humility, consideration of others, discipline, and honesty.
- The Taj Group prefers to recruit employees from the hinterland because that is where traditional Indian values still hold sway.
- Hire straight out of high school. Do not scout for the best English speakers or math wizards, look for three character traits: respect for elders (how does he treat his teachers?); cheerfulness (does she perceive life positively even in adversity?); and need (how badly does his family need the income from a job?).
- The chosen few are sent to the nearest of six residential Taj Group skill-certification centres, located in the metros. The trainees learn and earn for the next 18 months, staying in no-rent company dormitories, eating free food, and receiving an annual stipend of about 5,000 rupees a month in the first year, which rises to 7,000 rupees a month in the second year. Trainees remit most of their stipends to their families, because the Taj Group pays their living costs.
- One level up, the Taj Group recruits supervisors and junior managers from approximately half of the more than 100 hotel management and catering institutes in India. It cultivates relationships with about 30 through a campus-connect programme under which the Taj Group trains faculty and facilitates student visits. It maintains about 10 permanent relationships while other institutes rotate in and out of the programme.

- For the company's topmost echelons, the Taj Group signs up 50 or so management trainees every year from India's second- and third-tier B-schools such as Infinity Business School, in Delhi, or Symbiosis Institute, in Pune, usually for functions such as marketing or sales. It doesn't recruit from the premier institutions, as the Taj Group has found that MBA graduates from lower-tier B-schools want to build careers with a single company, tend to fit in better with a customer-centric culture, and aren't driven solely by money.
- Emphasis on training and mentoring, which helps to sustain its customer centricity.
- Most hotel chains train frontline employees for 12 months, on average, but the Taj Group insists on an 18-month programme. Managers, too, go through 18 months of classroom and on-the-job operations training.
- A Recognition-as-Reward System. Underpinning the Taj Group's rewards system is the notion that happy employees lead to happy customers. One way of ensuring that outcome, the organisation believes, is to show that it values the efforts of both frontline and heart-of-the house employees by thanking them personally. These expressions of gratitude, senior executives find, must come from immediate supervisors, who are central in determining how employees feel about the company. In addition, the timing of the recognition is usually more important than the reward itself.
- Using these ideas, in 2001 the Taj Group created a Special Thanks and Recognition System (STARS) that links customer delight to employee rewards.

Employees accumulate points throughout the year in three domains: compliments from guests, compliments from colleagues, and their own suggestions. Crucially, at the end of each day, a STARS committee comprising each hotel's general manager, HR manager, training manager, and the concerned department head review all the nominations and suggestions. The members of this group decide whether the compliments are evidence of exceptional performance and if the employee's suggestions are good then they post their comments on the company's intranet. If the committee doesn't make a decision within 48 hours, the employee gets the points by default.

- By accumulating points, Taj Group employees aspire to reach one of five performance levels: the managing director's club; the COO's club; and the platinum, gold, and silver levels. Departments honour workers who reach those last three levels with gift vouchers, STARS lapel pins, and STARS shields and trophies, whereas the hotel bestows the COO's club awards. At an annual organisation-wide celebration called the Taj Business Excellence Awards ceremony, employees who have made the Managing Director's club get crystal trophies, gift vouchers, and certificates.

- According to independent experts, the Taj Group's service standards and customer retention rates rose after it launched the STARS programme, because employees felt that their contributions were valued. In fact, STARS won the Hermes Award in 2002 for the best human resource innovation in the global hospitality industry. The Taj Group's hiring, training, and recognition systems have together created an extraordinary service culture, but you may still wonder if the response of the Taj Mumbai's employees to 26/11 was unique. Perhaps. Perhaps not.

Entrepreneurship

Nations must create an ecosystem of entrepreneurship if they wish to sustain high growth trajectory. What exactly is an enabling Entrepreneurship Ecosystem? The term (entrepreneurship ecosystem) was first coined by James Moore. He thought of entrepreneurship ecosystems as relationally embedded nature of firms interacting with customers, suppliers and financiers. A more comprehensive description would include existing and prospective entrepreneurial actors, organisations, institutions, processes, degree of sellouts – which formally and informally coalesce to connect, moderate and govern the performance within the local entrepreneurial environment. Daniel Isenberg propagated an enabling entrepreneurship ecosystem based on six broad factors. These include "a conducive culture, enabling policies and leadership, availability of appropriate finance, quality human capital, venture friendly markets for products, and a range of institutional supports." These generic domains comprise hundreds of elements interacting in highly complex and idiosyncratic ways. The data in the Table below establishes a clear correlation between entrepreneurship ecosystem and economic well being of nations:

Table

Country	*GDP 2000 $ billions*	*GDP 2020 $ billions*	*GDP per capita 2000 $*	*GDP per capita 2020 $*	**Entrepreneurship Ranking 2018/GEI*	
Brazil	655	1.4 Tn	3749	6790	98/20.3	
Russia	259	1.5 Tn	1771	10127	78/25.2	
India	468	2.6 Tn	443	1901	68/28.4	Major Changes during last three years
China	1.2 trillion	14.7 Tn	959	10500	43/41.1	Took off on exponential growth since 2004
South Africa	13.6	30 Bn	3032	5091	57/32.9	
Japan	4.8 trillion	5 trillion	38532	40113	28/51.5	
South Korea	576	1.6 trillion	12256	31489	24/54.2	
Singapore	92bn	339.9bn	23852	59798	27/32.7	
Israel	132	401	21101	43611	16/65.4	
Pakistan	79bn	263	576	1194	120/15.6	Major deterioration since 1993

**The GEI ranking is based on a mix of attitudes, resources, and infrastructure generally known as the entrepreneurship 'ecosystem'. It also includes abilities, and aspirations of the local population, broadband connectivity and the transport links to external markets. The Global Entrepreneurship Index (GEI) is based on fourteen factors – opportunity perception, start-up skills, Degree of Fear of Failure, Networking, cultural support, opportunity to start up, tech sector, quality of human capital, competition, new product, new technology, high growth, information system, risk capital.*

Source: See end notes.

So Whom Should We Follow?

We now come back to the question, 'whom should we follow?' The realistic answer is, "none", follow the major principles of political economy of our ancient past when India remained an economic and military powerhouse for two millennium. Yes we must adapt the execution to the current global environment.

Vasudhaiva Kutumbakam, Ekatmvad and Relevance of Chanakya for India

The Bhartiya philosophy of human life and ultimate goal of all humans (and perhaps living being) is final samadhi into the Creator of the cosmos. Thus, all beings are one. Translated into economic activity gain of one human or a country or society need not be loss of another. No zero-sum game in two or multiple players involved in an activity. In modern term it has to be win-win for all. Include in this equation the environment (planet earth and the outer space) the picture becomes more comprehensive. It is the Creator who has given this universe to us for planning our temporal and physical journey. Everything that is taken from the universe needs to be with due caution. What we take must be replenished. If not done by human activities, then the Mother Nature will step in with the destructive force to take it back.

Hence when we define the best marketing person as one who can sell a fridge to an Eskimo, we go wrong. Creating need where it does not exist will be problematic. The Eskimo in the instant case is being cheated and most probably the fragile eco system in which they live is likely to be damaged. Similarly growing big, bigger and the biggest swallowing the smaller entities is likely to boomerang. Infact Adam Smith (*The Wealth of Nations*) was dead against corporatisation and big corporates in 1776. Since Smith treated economic activities as part of moral science. Hence human morality with respect to fellow human beings and also with respect to nature was key to morally correct economic activity. We will come back to this in the context of Chanakya's philosophy of political economy and human character.

The concept of *ekatmvad* is best explained by the *ashtang* yoga description. When India proposed Yoga as an international practice almost all countries accepted this wholeheartedly. So, the yogaasana became very popular. But Yoga is much more than those physical asanas. The eight parts of Yoga are *Yama*, *Niyama*, *Asana*, *Pranayam*, *Pratyahar*, *Dharana*, *Dhyan* and *Samadhi*. For our purpose a brief description and relevance of *yama* would suffice. *Yama* entails non-violence, truthfulness, no stealing (others right), celibacy and avoid hoarding (anti-consumerism). All these parts of *Yama* are for the society and Nature in which all beings live. Thus the primary duty of all beings is first to the society and the universe before they focus on themselves (*niyam*, *asana* etc.). If we revisit the earlier discussion on modern economy then the emphasis needs to be on strengthening the MSMEs and even individual small shopkeeper to survive. Make these millions of small entities more productive and useful rather than coax them to grow in size. This incidentally gels with the concept of supply chain management where thousands of small entities collaborate and cooperate in delivering product or service without any entity controlling the other. The trick here is management of the supply chain as against controlling or monopoly of the supply chain. We can now look at the *Arthashastra*.

The first Indian treatise on political economy was written by Kautilya about 300 BC in *Arthashastra* – collection of economic principles from one of the ancient vedas – the Atharveda which goes back several centuries before the *Arthashastra*. Kautilya in *Arthashastra*, listed seven constituent elements of a nation. The 'forces' – of defence, law and order, rank at sixth after the King, councilors, territory, fortified towns, treasury (wealth of the state). Thus, during the period when India was at the top in terms of economic and military power economy took precedence over the military power (Rangarajan, p. 97). At the same time Chandragupt and his several successors also maintained one of the strongest armed forces in the world to protect the wealth of the state. The wealth creators formed an important institution of the state that helped the king to maintain the military for protecting all the constituent elements of the state. They were given great status in the kingdom.

It is generally accepted that a rich and growth-oriented corporate environment enhances some of the major factors of competitive advantages to a nation. These include facilitating proactive foreign policy, projection of soft and hard power, creation of new knowledge and skills, catalyzing human productivity, inculcating collaborative culture, strengthening internal harmony and so on.

Economic productivity was so important in ancient India that Kautilya envisaged two types of habitats for the citizens – those who were exempted to pay taxes (and hence not involved in economic productive activities) and citizens who were economically productive. The reason for this segregation was the fear that citizens with capability to be economically productive are likely to become lazy and unproductive in the company of those who were not economically productive. Adam Smith in, '*The Wealth of Nations*' also emphasises the importance of a citizen's efficiency and productivity.

Some of the major tenets of Kautilya's economic policy were as under:

- The quantum of taxation for all was one sixth (around 16 percent) of the earnings.

- Most people paid taxes and this included the farmers and those involved in agriculture.
- Kautilya advised free trade with slightly higher taxes on those wealth creators who were involved in foreign trade.
- The kingdome encouraged use of state produced goods and services wherever possible.
- It was also the time when the Indian goods and services (education, health care etc.) were the best in the world.
- Poor farmers who were below subsistence level were exempted from paying taxes. Instead, the king gave them additional help and resources to increase their productivity. The period for which this help was given was for four years. After this period the concerned citizen was expected to increase his economic productivity and start paying taxes. If he failed, he was punished by the king.
- Citizens had duties towards the State – in terms of national security (reporting anti-state activities) and for supporting economy of the state by being economically productive.
- The king was responsible for creating physical infrastructure, health care, security of individual citizen and education. Thus roads, water bodies, wells, resting places for the travelers were constructed by the knig.
- Spiritual people, those involved in study and dissemination of scriptures were not expected to pay any tax. Instead, their proper subsistence levels were maintained by the king. However, fakes and cheats were punished.

- The judicial system and law enforcing agencies were alert, just and prompt in delivering justice and maintaining law and order in the kingdom.
- The king was expected to be a person of strong character– devoid of lust, anger, bias, greed.
- Kautilya understood the inter relation between the wealth of a nation (*Kosa* or treasury) and the forces (*danda*) hence the word 'Kosadanda' keeping the treasury (*Kosa*) and the army (*danda*) together

However, Kautilya wrote the *Arthashastra* for an imaginary ideal State. It will be safe to assume that bulk of the directions in the *Arthashastra* were followed by Chandragupt and the subsequent rulers for several centuries. This was the time when India was the richest and most powerful nation in the world.

Role of Corporate Leadership and Corporate Performance Metrics

Considering the fact that these wealth creators are considered as important if not more than the wealth protectors (Kautilya's concept of Kosa danda) the leadership at different levels is as important as is the case with military leadership.

Jim Collins (*Good to Great*) prescribed some major leadership approaches. The top leader in these organisation need to be self-effacing, quiet, reserved and even shy, with personal humility and rock-solid resolve to pursue professionally correct approach. He called them level five leaders. These leaders tend to leave a lasting legacy much beyond their respective tenures with the enterprise. In one of 'HBR's 10 Must Reads' – written, 'On Leadership' Jim Collins describes the other levels (from one to four) of leadership from highly capable individual graduating to contributing to the team, competent managers, effective leader and finally the level five leader labeled as 'executive' by him. The highly skilled individual has talent, knowledge, skills and good work habits. The next level helps in achieving group objectives. The competent manager ensures effective and efficient pursuit of objective. The level four leader ensures strong commitment to vigorous pursuit of clear and compelling vision. These great organisations must focus on people with character, skills are easy to impart while character needs very long-time frame for transformation. Their third major feature is absolute realism in accepting the degree of difficulty in achieving the goals and unwavering faith in ultimate success. Finally, these breakthrough organisation do not pursue technology at the cost of their core competence. Instead, they exploit technology to further their goals.

The WEF in the era of fourth industrial revolution anticipates a very different tone of leadership. In fast changing business environment due to several factors ranging from customers' preferences, new technologies, sudden set-backs and so on the emphasis needs to be elevating people rather than replacing them. Greater emphasis needs to be on truth, trust, and transparency. Long hierarchies prevalent during the command-and-control era need to be dismantled. Leaders who can be good influencers at functional levels need to be nurtured and empowered. There is need for continuous upgradation of digital skills across the organisation. Organisations need to create intrapreneurs within their organisation by allowing the employees to innovate with focus on business growth, accept mistakes and tap the creativity of each leader. Given the fast pace of business growth and changes the era of spending time on completing pilot projects before starting with the main project needs to be replaced by progress and achieve perfection on the job. Lastly the challenges of inequalities need to be addressed by business leaders by addressing social tensions and protection of environment. There needs to be a new drive to extend the benefits to the families from the individuals and then to the societies. The leaders in the fourth industrial revolution need to be inspirational, innovative, advocate humanity, collaborate within and outside the organisation, orchestrate growth by empowering and enabling and embrace change with enthusiasm.

The Economic Roadmap for Vision 2047

The above discussion on the political economy for achieving the goals of Vision 2047 brings out some specific action plans;

- Do not follow the West but assimilate our ancient wisdom (*ekatmvad* and Kautilya's *Arthashastra*) suitably adapted to the current environment.
- Think big not in quantum but in quality low cost and zero defect, think of enriching the nation.
- Identify, train and retain talent. If it is not available get involved in training and skilling activities.
- Create and sustain an ecosystem of entrepreneurship.
- Collaborate, cooperate and compete globally to create values – profits will follow.
- Ensure value for money and value for human labor. Wasting money is a sin, wasting human endeavor is a greater sin.

- People matter, but good people matter much more. If good people are not available create them with character building, training and enabling ecosystem.
- In the four quadrant of BCG matrix (dog, cash cow, star and question mark) the big businesses must focus more on the star and question mark. To do this they will have to invest in R&D.
- Create new technologies – such as quantum computing, cyber security, AI, robotics, precision science, Artificial Intelligence, alternatives to rare earth minerals and fossil fuel,
- Focus on the dual use technologies and system that serve the twin purpose of creating national wealth and securing the nation.

Chapter Three

Military Power

Military Power in Geopolitics

Our popular understanding of military power is defined in terms of fighter aircraft (number of squadrons), tanks, guns, ammunition, number of soldiers and of course modern military technologies. To some extent all these do form part of this power – but a very small part. Because, if this was military power Israel would have never won, the US must have never lost, the USSR must have never disintegrated, Vietnam should never have won.

In modern knowledge society or in the age of information war a nation has several components to achieve its desired geopolitical goals. Political, economic, narrative and net wars are in non-military domain. Physical destruction, psychological war, command and control war, military deception, electronic war and so on are in the military domain. Military scholars have also coined a number of other war forms in the military domain – these are more academic in nature and some are just semantics.

Most important aspect that ensures successful use of military power is over all efficiency and synergy among political and military leadership, capability of the force itself in delivering the results in shortest possible time with minimal collateral damage and the technostructure that supports the military power. The top political leaders are expected to identify what to protect – values, citizens and territory. The military leadership is expected to derive correct military goals form the political goals and stage manage the force in the cognitive and physical domain. The force itself needs to display courage, adaptability and precision. Ideally application of military power needs to be for shortest possible time window in which all the military objectives are achieved. From here on the political leadership takes over to ensure that the military achievements are exploited to attain the geopolitical position.

In the context of our discussion we will address three major aspects of military power. First major reforms at cultural and organisational levels. Second our quest for self-reliance in military power (technostructure), transforming political economy so that military expenditure is turned into investment and finally the synergy of application of military power in conjunction with other components of national power.

The Biggest Organisational and Cultural Reforms in the Indian Armed Forces

During the World War II the Allied and the Axis powers organised their armed forces in Unified Regional Theatre Command on the principles of unity of command and clear enunciation of authority, accountability and resource utilisation. Today more than 32 nations have Unified Theatre Commands. Indian armed forces waited for these most obvious and necessary reforms for more than seven decades until the political leadership made it mandatory for them in 2020 by appointing the first Chief of defence Staff. The Indian Parliament got involved in the process by introducing the Inter Services Organisations (Command Control and Discipline) Bill 2023 on 15 March 2023. The reforms that will cover jointness, integration and structures (creating regional theatres) are still work in progress. It will be very realistic to accept that the Indian armed forces did have several reservations against these reforms. Bulk of these reservations are a reflection of the British Indian Armed Forces legacy.

During recently concluded Operation SINDOOR inter-Service synergy was visible. However this was a 88-hour affair. Taking Operation SINDOOR as validation of the fact that Indian Armed Forces have learnt the art and science of joint planning and execution will be stretching our optimism too far. We must also be realistic in accepting that Operation SINDOOR had very limited objectives. The astounding victory in this operation has not achieved any geopolitical goal. On the contrary it has just set the stage for a bigger military conflict where India will have to be on its own without any Russian or American support. Whereas our adversary is likely to get support from the US and even China. What can be such major conflicts? What are likely to be our shortcomings if we fight in the old ways taught to us by our British Military officers (Ismay, Mountbatten and all). Some examples from the World War II and our performances in 1965, 1971 will be helpful in understanding the goals and limitations.

In the battle of France against 138 French Infantry Divisions (including the British Expeditionary Force – BEF) the Germans had just 131. Against 3173 tanks of the French (including 310 British tanks) the Germans had 2445. In terms of combat aircraft also the Allied Forces had more than those of the Germans. Second, the quality of major equipment like the tanks, artillery pieces, and aircraft also gave advantage to the Allied Forces. It took less than two weeks for the Germans to defeat this force. The Germans covered the distance from the start point – Ardennes, to the finish line – Dunkirk, more than 200 kms. It was not because the Germans had better tanks, aircraft or other weapon system. On the contrary a large number of German tanks had machine guns as their main weapons. The French and the British tanks were all fitted with 75 mm guns – much more powerful than machine guns. The Germans used Stuka Dive bombers which were easy targets for the British Spitfire. But while the Stukas were supporting the German advance with close air support the Spitfires were busy fighting their air war somewhere else.

We need to remember that the British had trained the Indian armed forces. Lord Mountbatten and Lord Ismay had prepared the war doctrine for India's military in 1947. This doctrine prevailed in India till 1963. As a contrast the Israeli Defense Forces (IDF) had fought alongside the Allied Forces (under the British Command) during World War II. The two Israeli brigades that formed part of the Israeli military in this war formed the nucleus for raising the IDF in 1948. The very first action David Ben Gurion took on forming the IDF was to discard all the doctrinal and tactical teachings of the British. As per him the British were habitual of fighting set piece battles. Ben Gurion knew for sure that in war there are no set piece battles. Churchill who did provide political (and very often military!) leadership to the British forces in World War II found the British commanders slow, plodding and bereft of imagination. If we study the Israeli campaigns against the Arabs – 1948, 1956, 1967, 1973 and even 2016 they fought more like the Germans and never fought like the British.

In 1965, India's Western Command with around ten divisions against around six divisions of Pakistan planned to advance up to (and not beyond!) Ichhogil canal. The distance from the International Border to the canal at the maximum being less than 30 kms. By the end of the War the Western Command had just reach there. The General Officer Commanding in Chief Lt General Harbaksh Singh flags lack of inter-Service synergy as one of the reasons.

In 1971 while in the Eastern Theatre the Indian Forces outclassed all other global armed forces their performance in the Western (Shakargarh) and Southern (Jaisalmer) sectors was not up to the mark. In Shakargarh sector India's Western command could advance around eight kms against the planned objective of advancing to Pasrur – which was 80 kms from the International Border. In Southern Command the 11 Infantry Division did advance to Nayachor in Pakistan but the 12 Infantry Division refused to launch offensive even after Wing Commander (Later Air Marshal) Bawa had decimated the Pakistani offensive at Longewal.

Why are we discussing all this? Because of the simple reason that for replicating the performance of Operation SINDOOR at a larger scale we will have to unlearn what the British taught us and learn from our experience of Operation SINDOOR. This would entail whole hearted participation from top to bottom in embracing the tenets of unified theatre command. The reforms set in motion in the 2023 Bill are long overdue.

Indigenisation of Indian Air Force: A Case Study in Self-Reliance in Defence Production

Our critical deficiency in number of fighter squadrons is the most talked about subject when it comes to find gaps in indigenisation of defence resources. Thus our journey in equipping the air power and the present transformation would serve as a good case. On 15 August 1947 India inherited six squadrons of Spitfires (700 km per hour speed at 11000 ft, 2462 km operating range and powered by 2180 horse power engine) and Tempest (750 km per hour at 24500 ft) ground attack fighters. These were among some of the good performers around that time. In 1948 India procured the Vampires (835 km per hour) – heralding the age of jet fighters. In 1953, the French Ouragans (950 km per hour in level flight at height 15000 meters) were added to the IAF, followed by British Hawkers Hunters with speeds of .95 Mach (1150 km per hour), Gnat (1120 km per hour, 800 km range) Canberra bombers (933 km per hour at 48000 ft of height 3.5 tons of ordnance, could fly at heights of 10 km). As per the available literature on the subject India had 23 squadrons of combat aircraft in the early sixties. All these aircraft were modern as per the contemporary standards. In terms of number and quality India had the best air force in Asia when we fought the Chinese in 1962 (and did not employ IAF in combat role!!).

It was the first Indian Prime Minister who dared to dream really big with an ambition to make India the first country in Asia to produce its own fighter aircraft. He picked up a Nazi scientist – Kurt Tank, who had built the most successful German fighter aircraft – Folk Wulf Fw190 during the World War II. The IAF too dreamt big by asking for Mach 2 speed for this fighter. No fighter in the world had this speed in 1956! For the power train HAL was to develop its engine 'Kaveri', in collaboration with the Germans. The first prototype that flew in 1961 was powered by an Orpheus engine (used in Folland Gnat). Obviously the HF24 was subsonic. It was capable of carrying 1800 kg bombs, 100 rockets (68 mm) and four canons (30 mm). HF 24 took part in 1971 War with Pakistan, shot down a

Pakistani F86 Sabre on 7 December 1971, three pilots flying HF 24 in this war were awarded Veer Chakra. Though HF 24 had some glaring short comings. First when the fighter used all the four canons together the vibrations were so strong that the automatic flight control system of the aircraft stopped. The IAF lost a test pilot (Sqn Ldr Sapre) when he tried using all the four canons during operations in 1971. Its canopy used to fly off at some attack angles. Those who flew the plane found it a good war machine that could be improved upon (to meet the future needs of the IAF). But somehow the shortcomings were not (or could not be) removed. The last HF 24 flew in 1990. Thus, the HF 24 story became a mix of lofty goals, romanticism, commitment of India's air warriors with their now famous daring, raw courage and patriotism.

The Second Phase of Induction of Combat Aircraft: Many Countries Many Aircraft

The failure of HF 24 project triggered a long series of import of fighter aircraft from erstwhile USSR and later Russia, France and the UK. MiG-21 came to India in 1963 followed by Su 7, MiG-23, MiG-25, MiG-27, MiG-29, Su 30 MKI from Russia. From UK and France came Jaguars, Mirage 2000, Rafale. Three of these – MiG-23, 25 and 27 are out of service. Three squadrons of MiG-21 retired in August 2025. That would leave us with 28 squadrons. Five of these will comprise of the French made Mirage 2000 and Rafale – three and two squadrons respectively. Sixteen will be of Su30 MKI and MiG-29 – (thirteen and three respectively), five British Jaguar squadrons and two squadrons of indigenous Tejas. India fought the 1965 and 1971 wars with first generation aircraft except for MiG-21 which can be considered belonging to third generation. The current inventory of Indian aircraft with their modifications can easily qualify for fourth generation combat aircraft. Rafale is considered slightly ahead of fourth generation – generally referred as 4.5 generation!

This phase of equipping the IAF with supersonic fighter aircraft commenced in early eighties with British Jaguars (1980), Russian MiG-29 (1987) and Su30MKI (initially Su30 Mk 1) in 1997 Mirage 2000 in 1998, indigenously built Tejas in 2016 and finally French Rafale in 2021. The Su30MKI is the most versatile, powerful aircraft in the inventory. Besides its top speed of about Mach 2 at 11000 ft it has capability to track 20 aerial targets and attack eight of these simultaneously. It can act as mini-Air Borne Warning and Control System (AWACS) for four fighters in its team. It has been modified to carry a 2.5 tons BrahMos supersonic missile (Mach 2.8). It has the best in service avionics, RADAR, precision guidance system, electronic warfare pack, long endurance (can fly for ten hours with mid-air refuelling and hence can achieve an operating range of 8000 km). Bulk of the modifications in the aircraft have been done by HAL.

The French Mirage 2000 is an equally potent and proven strike aircraft (proved its worth in Kargil operations and in the Balakot strike). With a Mach 2.2 speed it is loaded with a host of guided weapons and Electronic Counter Measures. Its Electronic Warfare (EW) pack is indigenous. The Tejas at 1.6 Mach is considered superior to Mirage 2000 in combat role. The MiG-29 and MiG-29 K are air superiority aircraft have top speed of 2.35 Mach and are equipped with some of the latest guided weapons and electronic suits. The IAF and the IN are equipped with MiG-29. The Naval version is modified for short take off but assisted recovery. The Rafale at 1.8 Mach is considered the best multirole aircraft in its category. As per Dassault Aviation a single Rafale can perform the tasks that required seven French aircraft of earlier generation. Hence the French air force is replacing 700 aircraft of earlier generation with 225 Rafales!! The Jaguars (Mach 1.37) are oldest aircraft in this pack. However, with their inhouse modification Display Attack Ranging Inertial Navigation III (DARIN-III) these aircraft are likely to play useful role for more than a decade

The Curious Case of Tejas: Big Push for Indigenisation

It began in 1978 when Air Chief Marshal I.H. Latif (1978-81) was at the helm. Frustrated by the inability to fix the nagging shortcomings in HF 24 and poor performance of MiG-21 the IAF wanted a low-cost replacement for both these combat aircraft in a short time frame. The aeronautical engineers at the Hindustan Aeronautics Limited (HAL) wanted to showcase their prowess in design and approached the then Prime Minister late Mrs. Indira Gandhi. The Prime Minister agreed and asked them to produce a state of art combat aircraft. Accordingly, the IAF gave them the Air Staff Requirement (ASR). The ambitious project included fly by wire capability, composite material airframe, multifunctional display controlled by mission computer, multimode radar, guided air to air and air to surface weapons, and electronic warfare protection and a powerful jet engine (remember Kaveri?). Four organisations were to work on this as a team – the Hindustan Aeronautical Limited (HAL), Aeronautical Design Agency (ADA), Gas Turbine Research Establishment (GTRE) and of course the IAF. Given the ambitious goal it was evident that the 'futuristic' combat aircraft cannot be inducted by 1990. It was only in 2015 that the first set of Tejas were inducted in the IAF. This induction in a way was 'pushed' by the government.

The CAG, (in 'Performance Audit on Design Development Manufacture and Induction of Light Combat Aircraft') brings out some surprising and unflattering facts about the overall functioning of public sector and their users' participation in such a project of national importance. Firstly, the HAL and later the ADA, were exceptionally high on ambition and remarkably poor in knowledge-base, expertise and overall performance. Hence, they always failed to keep their own timelines. The IAF on their part behaved as a typical user. When the project commenced the IAF was asked to send their team of officers to form part of a 'Standing Liaison Group' as early as in 1989. It took them seventeen years to post their representatives to the group (when a Group of Ministers was formed to oversee the project) in 2006. The reason for this delay as per the IAF (reported in the CAG Performance Audit) was that IAF as a user can only be part the Standing Liaison Group once the aircraft design is finalised! The CAG was not satisfied by the response in the Report.

Thirdly, a project that was of national importance was dealt in bits and pieces – airframe by the ADA, manufacture by HAL, hardpoints for weapon systems by some other country, electronic warfare and radar component by another country and aeroengine by the GTRE of India. Thus, by the time the airframe design was finalised and prototype made, the IAF revised the weapons for the hardpoints (missile from R-60 to R-73, additional place for the Russian M-62 bomb, additional Derby and Python missiles in 2009). This made the design engineers to revisit the drawing board and hence further delay.

The GTRE on their part failed to provide the aeroengine that could power LCA. The engine lacked desired power, was too heavy, suffered from excessive vibrations at higher altitudes was bigger than required in size. Hence, the GE F404 engine for the LCA. The initial lot of LCAs handed over to the IAF had 110 critical and 393 non-critical deficiencies. The user was told that HAL will remedy all the shortcomings. The IAF accepted 36 (two squadron) LCAs. As per a Government of India Press Release of 01 July 2023 all the shortcomings have been removed, Tejas is a multirole platform that ranks among the best in the class. It has taken part in a number of air shows in India and abroad. It is capable of maritime reconnaissance and strike roles, has enhanced manoeuvrability, is equipped with multimode airborne radar, self-protection suite and lasers designation pods. The press release also sites the additional order for 83 Tejas by the IAF as proof of users' confidence in the LCA. However, all engines for the 83 aircraft will be given by the GE (F404 and F414).

Strategic Shift in Political Economy from Defence Expenditure to Defence Investment

There is a need for transformation in the cognitive approach, organisational structures and cultures and corresponding reforms in processes. Thus, we need to think of defence investment as against defence expenditure. Secondly, starting ratios do not decide the outcome of wars. Thirdly, create competitive market conditions and lastly adopt a 'whole of the nation' approach.

Expenditure to Investment. The size of global market for defence related products in 2024 is 2494 billion dollars. This is expected to reach 3871 billion dollars by 2033 at 5 percent annual growth. Even the Indian defence market in 2024 is US $ 17.2 billion – expected to reach US $ 28.4 billion in 2033. Back in the 1970s when India had developed HF 24 Marut the Eastern African countries wanted to import this aircraft. India did not favour export of weapons

– perhaps due to their ideal of non-violence. There is a need to get real and shun this misplaced belief. Fortunately, during the past few years exports of Indian weapon systems are on the increase. The national leadership is enthusiastic about increasing such exports. The LCA itself was showcased in several countries and there appears to be sizable demand for this low-cost high-grade combat aircraft. The global market for military aircraft in 2025 is US $ 50.59 billion expected to grow more than US $70 billion in 2032. For Commercial aircraft the market size is US $ 157.3 billion expected to reach US $ 260 billion by 2033. Even the aeroengine market for production and Maintenance Repair Overhaul (MRO) for military aircraft for the next two decades would be US $ 6.7 billion for India (2000 military aircraft). For commercial aircraft for the next two decades, it would be around US $ 128 billion. Incidentally, India would be procuring 1350 horse power engines (replacing the 1000 HP engine) for the Russian T 90 tanks we have a huge demand for automobiles, rapidly expanding navy, thus the overall payoffs for investing in the mobility market in terms of jobs creation, impetus to GDP and international clout would be extremely attractive. However, we will have to set up our own benchmarks that are realistic and help gradual indigenisation. Remember there was no need to peg the HF 24 speed at Mach 2. There was no need for four canons if their simultaneous use rattled the aircraft control system. Today we need to think and critically analyse the urgency of 42 squadrons. We have Rafale, Su30 MKI, MiG-29s, Mirage 2000s and LCAs. The Su30 MKI engines – that have a thrust of 126 KN per engine, are sourced through an Indian company. More than 50 percent of the engine is indigenous. Russia is keen to give an upgraded version of this engine that can produce 146 KN. Around 240 of these engines (126KN) are being procured. Given the capabilities of Su 30 MKI, India gets additional time of perhaps one to two decades to produce their own indigenous aero engine that meets our requirements and helps us get a reasonable share of the market.

From Monopoly to Perfect Competition

The defence production units – till very recently, remained in monopolistic silos. Hence, we remained the top importers of defence systems from abroad in spite of our declared policy of indigenisation way back in 1967. It was in 2017 that 41 ordnance factories were merged into seven Defence Production Public Sector Units doing away with 246 years old rules and systems. In addition, the private sector was slowly brought at par with these DPPSUs to bid for defence projects. The case of developing an indigenous combat aircraft and an aeroengine that can generate 110 to 130 Kilo Newton thrust by HAL, ADA and the GTRE; suggests that more needs to be done to fully unshackle the great entrepreneurial spirits of the Indians – like we have done in developing our own cryogenic engine, nuclear reactors and fast breeders. Even in the military aircraft ecosystems HAL has excelled in producing indigenous combat helicopters such as Dhruv, Rudra and most recently Light Combat Helicopter (LCH) Prachand that can support land operations at heights around 16500 feet. For a long time, we were waiting for a replacement of Bofors. It was L&T of India in collaboration with South Korea that produced a gun far superior to Bofors. Our public sector organisations like the GTRE, HAL and ADA lacked resolute leadership, unwavering commitment, clarity of goal, team work. Besides excessive and unnecessary secrecy, bureaucratic red tapes, sticking to the rules rather than changing the rules where these obstruct achievement of goals resulted in wastage of money, delays and created a culture of subpar performance. There is a need to further open the defence industry to the private sector to create a level playing field for fair competition. The public sector units are a trove house of expertise and experience. They need to be given wings to fly in a competitive eco system.

For the first time since independence India inducted big ticket indigenous weapon platforms and systems to include medium guns, radars and surveillance systems, battle tanks, rifles, night vision devices, fighter aircraft, combat helicopters, trucks, armoured personnel carriers and so on. The private sector contribution in defence sector has been increasing every year. The preferential treatment given to public sector undertakings was removed. Instead, the public sector undertakings commenced hand holding and assisting the private sector enterprises in manufacturing some of the most complex defence systems.

The role of Medium and Small Enterprises (MSMEs) was recognised. The three services became facilitators in letting the MSMEs and industry in general know what they actually wanted. The MSMEs were encouraged to get in touch with the end users to understand the finer aspects of the products they wanted. The government earmarked 25 percent of the Research and Development funds for the industries. Portals like IDex (innovation in defence excellence) and Srijan (one stop portal for getting to know the defence sector requirements) were hosted for the prospective vendors. Meanwhile the structure, growth path and payment gateways for the small industries and start-ups were digitally networked and formalised.

On overall indigenisation front the Indian Defence Minister, said that 68 percent of the capital budget for defence is reserved for indigenous defence production. The Defence Research and Development Organisation (DRDO) has set up centres of excellence for young scientists. A total of 37 projects have been awarded to various industries mainly in the MSME sector. Government plans to fund at least 250 start-ups in the defence sector. The Prime Minister commissioned India's indigenously developed and built aircraft carrier Vikrant – with a new Indian Navy Flag dedicated to the memory of Chhatrapati Shivaji. This ship is almost one and a half times in size compared to the earlier Vikrant. This is the biggest ship India has built so far. Net import content that was 41.81 percent in 2018-19 has come down to 36 percent in 2020-21. This is closer to 'not more than 30 percent import' envisioned in 1967.

Macro Economy and Defence Modernisation

China spends around 1.5 percent of its GDP on defence that amounts to US $ 245 billion. This is equivalent of the total Plan outlay for India. Obviously competing with China in defence expenditure is not an option. More importantly India does not have to adopt this option in the interest of her national security. While maintaining a judiciously created military strength and displaying the will to use it if the situation demands, there are other fronts which are more important. These include an astute and pragmatic foreign policy, a robust economic growth trajectory, concerted efforts to compete for a place in the global supply chain and countering Chinese narrative war internally and in the international fora.

Where did we Faulter? Opportunities for the Future

As we analyse the facts described in the discussion above some pertinent inferences are obvious. During the last seven decades, France has progressed from Ouragan to Rafale; the US, Russia and even China have graduated from the so called first generation to sixth-generation combat aircraft while we are still looking for suitable engines for our combat aircraft. These countries that are spending enormous amount of capital on defence are also among the top exporters of defence systems. One of the prime reasons for this lead is their investment on research and development that gives them early access to niche technologies. As per World Bank Data (2021) China spent 2.43 percent of its GDP on R&D, where as we spent 0.65 percent. The Chinese private sector contributed three fourth to this investment while in case of India the private sector contribution was less than one-third. Given the fact that China's GDP itself is more than thrice that of India this is a huge gap. A small country like Israel spends close to 6 percent of its GDP on R&D. The US – the biggest exporter of defence systems and technologies to the world, spent 3.46 percent whereas France from whom we bought Rafale spent 2.2 percent on R&D in the same year. If we want to be Atmanirbhar in the future we need to invest in the future. Bulk of this investment in the future must come from the private sector that wishes to compete in global market. Secondly, our decision making gets influenced by external or self-generated narratives and ignores the facts. The HF24 was always a better option than MiG-21 in peace as well as in war. Throughout its service we lost much less HF24 compared to MiG-21s and even other foreign origin aircraft. Bulk of the HF24 losses were during war. Whereas very large number of its replacement aircraft (MiG-21) were lost in peace.

While People's Liberation Army Air Force (PLAAF) is equipped with its own indigenous aircraft we are dependent on number of countries for combat aircraft and even for the Maintenance Repair and Overhauls (MRO). It is time we stick to the indigenous LCAs and Advance Medium Combat Aircraft (AMCA) with indigenous aero engines even if this means waiting for another decade. It is also important to avoid getting stuck with the 'sixth-generation' narrative. A careful look at the differentiators between one generation to the another would indicate that except for the stealth technologies (related to shape and material) everything else is a function of Artificial Intelligence, software and information fusion. India has demonstrated leadership in these fields. India's success in launching its GSLV D5 with indigenous cryogenic engine in January 2014 proves the prowess of Indian scientists and engineers. The Indian rocket engine happens to be the lightest (though it carried much lighter payload – five tons) and more importantly of least cost of US $ 40 million compared to the next best Chinese engine costing US $ 56.5 million.

Post-2017 import commenced decreasing. India conducted two small but very effective operations against Pakistan – surgical strike in Uri sector and air strike in Balakot in Pakistan with modern weapon systems as good if not better than the adversary. Against China, India could deploy around 50,000 troops equipped with modern weapon systems and more than adequate logistic support – winter clothing and living accommodation, road infrastructure with supply back up.

The induction of Tejas into IAF provides an interesting case study when contrasted with earlier attempt to induct HF 24-Marut. To start with CAG found many shortcomings in the Light Combat Aircraft (LCA) project culminating in the production of Tejas. However, ignoring the CAG audit report, Tejas Mk I aircrafts were inducted in service. The Government announced ambitious plans to replace all the MiG-21s, 29s, Jaguars, Mirage 2000s with Tejas Mk II in the near future. In addition, India would be developing its own fifth-generation fighter aircraft. A number of countries have shown interest in buying Tejas from India. In 2022 the IAF ranked third on the world air power index in terms of fighting strength behind the US, Russia and ahead of Chinese air power.

Compare this with the HF 24 programme some six decades back. Envisioned in the 1960s, test flown by the IAF in 1967, took part in 1971 war with Pakistan, shot down a Pakistani F86 Sabre on 7 December 1971, three pilots flying HF 24 in this war were awarded Veer Chakra. The aircraft was shelved soon after!! Then began a quest for imported fighter aircraft from all over the world.

Overall the defence production for the financial year 2024-25 – as declared by India's Defence Minister (*TOI* 10 August 2025) has increased to 1.5 lakh crore. This marks 18 percent growth over the previous year. When compared to the year 2019-20 the defence production of 2024-25 has shown a remarkable growth of 90 percent. These are the fruits of creating a strong defence industrial base involving the public and private sector in collaborative, cooperative and at the same time competitive mode. In 2024-25 the defence exports have increased to ₹ 23,622 crore. While the PSUs accounted for 77 percent of total production the share of private sector increased from 21 percent to 23 percent. On 15 August 2025 the Prime Minister declared commencement of the production of indigenous combat aircraft. This is very big announcement – heralding an era of fighter jet engine production in India. Finally the Kavery engine has arrived. It is likely that a major chunk of avionics, Electronic Warfare suite, missile systems, guided bombs and aircraft material will also be indigenous. This will be a boost to defence production, defence exports and indigenisation of large number of IAF systems.

Chapter Four

Geopolitics

Military Power and Geopolitics

The classical concept of geopolitics was primarily based on geography in terms of capabilities of transportation, communications and destruction. This decided the character, number and locations of viable security units and systems in the emerging global international environment. This approach led to conflicts as nations competed with each other across global geography – especially in their projection of maritime power, to gain and maintain a position of relative importance. In fact, this created the Westphalian approach to international dominance – primarily a European approach. The Americans entered this competition with America for all of mankind, China pursued the middle kingdom approach of global domination, Iran and a few other countries, based on theological power structure, objected to the legitimacy of democratic government. According to them, the world needs to be ruled by Islamic theology. All these theories lead to persistent conflicts and war. To some extent this is what we see in the Russia-Ukraine War, Iran-Israel-US War, Chinese struggle for dominance, Israel-Iran and Israel-Palestine struggle and the Thailand-Cambodia War.

However, there is another approach to geopolitics that leads to peace and co-existence. This view promotes a global picture of political and economic relations. Here the strong and comparatively weaker country can also co-exist on mutually beneficial terms. They develop strategies based on international relations to counter a stronger country to exert influence in the area of interest in the weaker country. Economic relations and international trade play an important part. This approach also highlights the importance of cross-border businesses in stabilising relations among countries irrespective of their resource based power – or Comprehensive National Power (a term coined by the Chinese implying the factors based on which a country can dominate other countries).

With this as the background we can now come to the current geopolitical environment in which India will have to chart its strategies to achieve overall Vision 2047. S&P and KPMG have analysed the geopolitical dynamics of 2025. Their assessments bring out four types of threats. First, the high probability and high impact threats. These include cyber attacks, climate change and US-China tensions. Second, high impact but low probability risks – NATO-Russia relations and anti-globalisation. The other risks are energy security and dollar depreciation.

Energy and Climate Change. The turmoil in the Middle East, American sanctions against buying oil from Russia after the start of Ukraine-Russia War, American sanctions on Iran and the two wars in Iraq in 1991 and 2003 are all results of energy dominance. Given India's huge dependence on the oil-producing countries, energy security and geopolitical independence in pursuing its oil trade policy become critical. Climate change has become a very real existential threat for all nations – however adherence to the globally accepted policies has been rather poor especially by countries that default on rule of law behaviour.

Rise of nationalism and Protectionism. The days of global village have been overtaken by protectionism in international trade. This is especially so in agricultural products, textiles and other goods that do not require high technology inputs.

Exposure of weak links in the global supply chain post COVID-19. The US supported China in becoming the global manufacturing hub. This was done primarily to dominate Russia. However COVID-19 with its origin in China proved that the US has created a bigger threat to global trade with excessive dependence on China. There is competition amongst nations to replace China as an alternative supply chain. India has a big opportunity. But this will require a very rapid, reliable and competitive execution of right strategies. Given the speed at which Indian business has invested in R&D, scales, and quality, it is an uphill task.

Alarmingly high occurrences of cyber attacks sponsored by countries on their adversaries. Cyber attacks are routine activities amongst countries without any overt conflict. The US has been targeting countries in the European Union, India and of course China. Russia has launched cyber attacks on Estonia, Chechnya. Israel has done so against Syria and Iran. The peacetime cyber attacks have gained such notoriety that the issue has become an important point of discussion at the UN. India is targeted by China, Pakistan and even the US. These attacks impose economic costs. In the context of geopolitics India needs to create a foolproof cyber security apparatus as also capability to launch an appropriate cyber offensive if the need arises.

US-China relations in military power projections. As China becomes capable to challenge US dominance in geopolitics and initiate actions to operationalise its one-China policy by attacking Taiwan, a major conflict between these two top powers may disturb the prevailing equilibrium.

Complex and fragmented regulatory and tax environment. This creates unfair advantages for individuals and countries at the cost of other nations that follow the rules of international trade. While nations like the US, China and even Russia may indulge in taking punitive military actions, India will have to follow the rule of law and other non-military steps to safeguard its interests.

India's Geopolitical Challenges and Responses in the Volatile World Order

During the 79th Independence Day speech the Prime Minister dwelled on the geopolitical response on several aspects. The most direct response was on three issues. First, giving a clear signal to a traditional adversary on the Western border that any misadventure will be responded with much heavier punishment. Second, protecting India from internal threats – from air, space, cyber and demographic changes. Third, protecting India's agriculture, fisheries and animal husbandry. Fourth, a call for improving quality and cutting down the cost of manufacturing Indian goods.

Though India achieved a spectacular victory in Operation SINDOOR, it rattled two big powers – the US and China. The US administration came out openly in favour of Pakistan, China has always been anti-India and hence pro-Pakistan. India's emergence as the fastest growing economy, a serious contender to China in shifting the global supply chain and making Pakistan irrelevant militarily have placed India as a contender for global leadership. This position has its own costs. India has now to prepare to meet these geopolitical costs economically and if required militarily.

We have discussed the need to expedite large-scale reforms in the culture, organisational structure of the armed forces to herald an era of jointness in thinking, planning and execution. Also, the performance of Operation SINDOOR will have to be replicated on a much larger scale – swift, precise and of very high impact so that lasting peace is achieved after the employment of military tactics. Though this goal is best achieved by 'winning the war without fighting' the current international security environment and the belligerence of our neighbours may make military conflict very difficult to avoid.

Protecting Indian Infrastructure, Places of worship and Major Installations. The Prime Minister made an emphatic declaration of creating a protective envelop all around India – 'The Sudarshan Chakra', that will safeguard the critical infrastructure like the railways, banking, bridges and surface choke points, places of worships, command and control centres and important institutions from hostile actions. This involves several layers of security. First and foremost is securing the cyber space. This extends from the most basic to the most advanced components of the nation at three levels. These are the cognitive, software and physical levels. As per the global threat analysis in cyber space ransomware attacks are most prominent these days. However in India's case – given the inherent fault lines in the ecosystem such as exploiting sub-nationalities and theological aspects for winning elections to the extent of allowing illegal migrants in the country, the cyber threat will be more in the cognitive domain. This would involve creating a narrative of distrust, block reforms and tarnish India's image in international forum. Major efforts are being made in the field of cyber security. Quantum encryption techniques are being developed by the Indian firms for secure communications. Besides AI and Big Data tools are being developed to identify prospective cyber threats.

Government initiative in 'Innovation for Defence Excellence' (iDEX) and 'SRIJAN' have resulted in modern defence systems produced by the Indian start-ups – 'SWITCH UAV' by IdeaForge as a counter to drones, loitering ammunition by Alpha Design in collaboration with Elbit of Israel, and 'Nagastra I' by the Solar industries. 'New Space Research' has produced swarm drones. A Hyderabad based firm has developed 100 percent indigenous system (Indrajaal) that will protect an area 1000 to 2000 square kms against UAV, incoming weapons, loitering ammunition. It uses ten different technologies including cyber security, quantum computing, robotics and AI.

As a nation India may have to detach itself from the US technological supply chain and hence Indian industries will be required to invest heavily in developing own niche technologies. The days of quick profits would become history. The biggest payoff from this hard option would be technological leadership in the long run. The biggest challenge would obviously be the fact that corporate India is not prepared for it. The Government appears to be keen. It will have to transform the existing eco system by a series of timely nudges. If the Indian corporates succeed in doing so we will be far ahead of even China in times to come since the Chinese technological prowess was supported by the American tech companies and also by the American leadership.

It addition to the big corporate houses investing heavily into R&D for new technologies the MSMEs will have to transform in two major ways. First they will have to increase their efficiency and productivity manifolds. Gary Hamel and C K Prahalad in their bestselling book Competing for the Future bring out two very relevant factors for the Indian enterprises. Japanese, German and the US labour productivity was almost the same in 1986 (German labour productivity) slightly higher than both the US and Japanese labour productivity. By 1991 the Japanese labour productivity reached 150 per hour whereas the US and the German labour productivity reached slightly less than 120 per hour. In case of India our record of labour productivity is very dismal – ranked 133rd in the world. Ironically the Indian labour works 45.7 hours a week – highest in the globe. This needs to be studied and analysed. Norway with very relaxed work environment is among the first ten countries in the world by labour productivity. Our MSMEs need to work on this data. They have tremendous scope to increase their productivity by at least three times. With 63.3 million MSMEs trebling their productivity three times over their current production capacity we may get to the target in couple of years rather than waiting for a full decade!

Another factor for global competitiveness is related to resource leverage. The top nine companies (Gary Hamel, 2002) in terms of spending on R&D were all of American and European origin. Where top five companies topping US patent awards were all Japanese. Japanese companies as a rule spent much less than their American and European competitors in R&D and performed much better than their Western competitors. All quality gurus like W. Edward Deming, Joseph M. Juran and Philip B. Crosby were American citizens. Even Bill Smith – the six sigma inventor was American. All their teachings were best applied by the Japanese in the eighties and nineties.

The geopolitical strength needs to be citizen-centric. Thus as the nation gets rich the citizens must also be rich in comparison to the global population. They also need to be healthy and happy, well connected with the leadership. This is where Vision 2047 initiatives like e-guru, e-Vaidya etc. figure in. Our current levels of equality, satisfaction levels of citizens and citizen health would act as start lines. In terms of equality India ranks fourth (with a score of 25.5) in the world much ahead of communist China (35.7) and the, US (41.8). Please note that higher the figure more unequal the society. All these are World Bank figures. We can exploit this as a geopolitical leverage. However in overall competitiveness as per the World Economic Forum data of 2025 India is still far behind if viewed in terms of our global ambitions. India ranks 40th among 137 nations. Major concern areas are macro-economic environment (rank 80), health and primary education (rank 91), higher education (rank 75) technology readiness (rank 107) labour and market efficiency (rank 75). The silver linings are in innovation (29), institutions (39) business sophistication (rank 39) and market size (rank 3). If we go into the details of each of the twelve pillars the magnitude of the efforts needed to create and sustain a strong geopolitical posture will become very clear. The brighter side as per the WEF is that since 2014 India has made consistent improvements in most of the critical factors.

One of the most frequently asked question these days is 'how the tariff war launched by the current US administration – specifically targeting India going to affect us? Can we survive this? There is no denying the fact that India could have gained a lot from strategic partnership with the US. In the short run – if the US high tariffs are not lowered, Indian economy will definitely be affected. In the long run with the current state of India's resilient and growing economy India is going to benefit and thrive and it is the US economy that is going to be hit.

India is a leading partner in the BRICS nations. With 3.3 billion population BRICS contribute 37.3 percent to the global GDP outperforming the Group of seven nations. China (part of the BRICS) contributes 19.5 percent to the global GDP, India ranked second among the BRICS nations contributes 8.23 percent. The BRICS alliance is expanding. Indonesia, Iran, UAE, Egypt, Ethiopia have already joined. Thailand and Malaysia have shown interest in joining the bloc. The current tariff volatility is likely to push more nations in the ambit of BRICS. More importantly one-third of the oil producing nations are with BRICS. If Saudi Arabia finally decides to join the balance will be highly tilted in favour of this bloc. With China's initiative of New Development Bank and India's push for trading in the local currencies of the BRICS nations the geopolitical response to the US and the West will be strong. China has developed an alternative to international currency transfer through Society for Worldwide Interbank Financial Telecommunication (SWIFT), India's Unified Payments Interface (UPI) is another alternative to replace SWIFT. Since SWIFT is dominated by the US an alternative to this international payments will challenge the US currency and banking monopoly.

India's exports in July 2025 have been record high. Thus high tariffs have not affected India so far. It could just be that the Indian exporters expedited the exports to the US to beat the tariff deadline. India's exports to the US has been all time high in 2024. Major items that India exports include engineering goods, electronics, pharma products (generic medicines), gems and jewellery, petroleum products and RMG cotton. If India devices better manufacturing processes that improve quality and cut down costs the tariff barriers can very easily be surmounted. The imports from the US comprise of mineral fuels and oil, pearls and semi-precious stones, nuclear reactor boilers and electrical machineries. None of these are high value chain commodities. Though it is possible for India to find alternative markets for its exports and imports it is more advisable to maintain the US as a trading partner by cutting costs of products that are being exported and increase the volume of imports for products like oil and electrical. The US has been a major importer from India for a long time.

Meanwhile the rating agencies like S&P have upgraded India's rating to BBB. They have also maintained that given the effective money control and fiscal policies India is a long term safe destination for investment. The high US tariff are not likely to affect India's growth. They have also given better ratings to Indian banks. Thus cost of international credit for India is likely to be lowered.

Militarily we would have benefited by the US in the defence production and research but if the US tariff become unreasonable Indian indigenous R&D will improve thus giving a big boost to our indigenisation in defence production. As regards the Tejas Mk 1A project almost half a dozen Tejas Mk1A have successfully cleared their flight tests. More will join soon with the GE414 engines. India is close to developing their own fighter jet engines and is also in collaboration with SAFRAN of France. Our indigenous attack and utility helicopters have already proved better than the US counterparts.

We have a rich and tech savvy diaspora in the US. These Indian American citizens not only lead the American technology modernisation but have impact on the American elections. A pro-India narrative will have to be created to leverage this strength. Thus in addition to the American dollars that come to India from these rich American Indians the geopolitical heft will have to be created by these US citizens of Indian origin.

We need to move towards multipolarity from a position of strength. This is where India's behaviour as a nation during COVID and natural disaster would help. Thus finding new markets for Indian goods that face high tariff from the US would become that much easier. Russia may emerge as a major trade partner since we import Russian oil and in turn can export pharma, steel, aluminium and even defence equipment to Russia. If this happens in Indian and Russian currencies the global impact would be that much more favourable for India and perhaps for the world.

Vision 2047 in terms of geopolitics posturing of India need to leverage our hard and soft power. The hard power would involve military strength, cyber and space technologies, missiles, surveillance networks, drone warfare and technical as well as human intelligence. The soft power would comprise of economy, culture, lifestyle and health, initiatives in protection of environment.

Hard Power

- **Sea Power.** Blue water navy has been the most effective force to project hard power during the classical era of geo politics. This is how the UK – a small island country, projected their influence globally. India has been steadily expanding its naval forces to project its military powers along our trade routes as also for geopolitics counter.

Thus Indian forces across the Malacca Straits, development of Andaman Nicobar as transit point (an alternative to Singapore), and sending Indian naval ships to South China Sea are initiatives in this direction. Besides Indian Naval presence in Cyprus, Greece and the Red Sea, Gulf of Persia are likely to be strengthened in times to come. It is quite likely that India may have more than two carrier groups – may be three or four to dominate the Indian Ocean and other areas.

- **Air Power.** Strategic air power is an important component to supplement and support blue water navy. Though at present India does lack requisite number of combat squadrons, the current expansion plans do envisage maritime long range combat aircraft both for surveillance and strike missions. The 29 squadrons that IAF has today are all capable of mid-air refueling and can carry strategic missiles like the BrahMos.

- **Ground Forces.** As regards the ground forces India has developed capabilities to counter China and Pakistan in a two front war. This is an essential geopolitics requirement.

- **Missiles.** Though China has the much larger component of missiles force, India is fast catching up. Besides Indian missiles force has demonstrated their capability in precision attacks in the face of Chinese missile defence system.

- **Space.** Space provides an excellent opportunity for dual use technologies – resources that can be used in peace and war. By developing anti-satellite systems India has demonstrated its political will to counter Chinese initiatives in militarisation of space. A large number of Indian start-ups are entering in this sector.

- **Drone warfare.** India's performance in Operations SINDOOR has demonstrated our intent and capability in this field. By announcing their initiative in creating drone based military and non-military systems India has opened up this niche sector to entrepreneurs in the defence and non-military sectors. This area has emerged as a low cost high returns sector for the young entrepreneurs.

Soft Power

- **Supply Chain Resilience.** This is one area where the government, industries and the people need to synergise their efforts. Our manufacturing is still far below the requisite levels both in terms of quality and quantity to match the national and global requirements.
- **Rupee trade to break the dollar hegemony.** India has made spectacular technology demonstration through UPI. Since most countries have more faith in the Indian democracy than on the Chines economic exploitation, the Indian platform for international transactions has better chance to succeed in comparison to the Chinese alternative to SWIFT. India has also initiated rupee trade with several countries. As per reports of International Bankers (2023) the IMF has accepted the Indian rupee as a potential international currency along with Chinese renminbi (RMB). The Reserve Bank of India has permitted 22 countries to open Special Vostro Rupee Account in India thus facilitating trade in rupees. Some of the important countries where rupee is accepted to some extent are Singapore, Malaysia, Indonesia, Hong Kong, Sri Lanka, UAE, Kuwait and Oman. Rupee is a legal tender in Nepal and Bhutan.
- **Culture.** India has not capitalised on the richest culture that the country has – in terms of magnificent

monuments depicting thousands of years of history, diversity of climate, languages, customs and traditions, religious and medical tourism and so on. India ranks 39th as per the WEF in Travel and Tourism Development. There is enough scope to be among the top three destinations for tourism. Our rich culture can be easily leveraged to counter hostile narrative and thus help our geopolitical strength.

Notes

Chapter One: Introduction

Ashok Pathak, *India's Strategies for Information War and Cyber Deterrence*, Vitasta Publishing Pvt (Vivekananda International Foundation) Ltd 2020 ISBN 9789386473875

Claude Arpi, *Tibet: The Last of a Free Nation India Tibet Relations 1947-62*, Part 1, Vij Books India Pvt Ltd, 2/19 Ansari Road, 2017, ISBN 9789386457219

Durga Das, *India From Curzon to Nehru and After*, Rupa Publication Pvt Ltd, 7/16 Ansari Road Daryaganj New Delhi First Published 1969, Fourteenth Impression, 2022, ISBN 9788171675913

French Patrick, *Liberty or Death India's Journey to Independence and Division*, Harper Collins Publishers India, 1997, ISBN 8172233280

Gandhi Mihir, 'The Indian Payment Handbook 2023-2028', https://www.pwc.in/assets/pdfs/consulting/financial-services/fintech/publications/the-indian-payments-handbook-%E2%80%93-2023%E2%80%932028.pdf

India can become 10 trillion economy by 2032, *Economic Times* (21 Sep 2024) https://economictimes.indiatimes.com/news/economy/indicators/india-can-become-10-tn-economy-by-2032-beat-us-china-in-manufacturing-report/articleshow/113546156.cms?from=mdr

M J Akbar, *Tinderbox: The Past and Future of Pakistan*, Harpers Collins Publishers India, 2011, ISBN 9789350290392

Maulana Abul Kalam Azad, *India Wins Freedom* (The Complete Version) Orient Black Swan, 3-6-752, Himayat Nagar, Hyderabad, First Published 1959, Reprint 2022, ISBN 9788125005148

Menezes SL, *Fidelity and Honour: The Indian Army from the Seventeenth to Twenty-first Century*, Oxford University Press 1999, ISBN 0195650476.

Ministry of Consumer Affairs Food and Public Distribution 2022-23, https://www.pib.gov.in/PressReleasePage.aspx?PRID=1837078

Ministry of External Affairs, Govt of India – Vaccine Supply, 15 June 2023, https://www.mea.gov.in/vaccine-supply.htm

Research Areas in Space May 2025, https://www.isro.gov.in/media_isro/pdf/programme/Research_Areas_Space_Doc2025.pdf

Research Unit Press Bureau of India, 10 June 2025, Information https://static.pib.gov.in/WriteReadData/specificdocs/documents/2025/jun/doc2025610567801.pdf

Shashi Tharoor *An Era of Darkness: The British Empire in India*, Aleph Book Company, 7/16 Ansari Road Daryaganj, 2016, ISBN 9789383064656

The Guardian Editorial, 18 May 2014, 'India: Another Tryst with Destiny' 'https://www.theguardian.com/global/2014/may/18/india-narendra-modi-election-destiny

Virmani Arvind, Working Paper NITI Aayog, July 2024, https://www.niti.gov.in/sites/default/files/2024-07/WP_Viksit_Bharat_2024-July-19.pdf

Chapter Two: Economy

Adam Smith, *The Wealth of Nations*, Bantam Dell, New York, 2003, ISBN 0553585975

Ajay K Sood, Indian Institute of Corporate Affairs Study of 1000 companies R&D Expenditure (29 July 2024) https://psa.gov.in/CMS/web/sites/default/files/publication/Study%20of%20Top%201000%20Listed%20Companies_R%26D%20Expenditure.pdf

Amitabh Tiwari, *NDTV*, 28 Jan 2025, https://www.ndtv.com/opinion/why-over-half-of-all-itr-filings-in-india-are-zero-tax-7579295

C D Sahay (Editor), *A Political Economic Approach to Reclaiming India* (VIF Perspective) Vitasta Publishing Private Ltd, 2019

Collins Jim Built to Last Successful Habits of Visionary Companies Random House Business Books, 2005, ISBN 9781844135844

Cumulative number of vaccine doses administered for the coronavirus (COVID-19) across India from January 2021 to October 2023, https://www.statista.com/statistics/1202066/india-daily-cumulative-vaccine-doses-administered-for-covid-19/

David H Holt (James Madison University), *Entrepreneurship New Venture Creation*, Prentice Hall of India, New Delhi, 2004, ISBN 81-203-1281-3

December 2024 Crude Steel Production and 2024 global crude steel production totals (24 January 2025) Brussels https://worldsteel.org/media/press-releases/2025/december-2024-crude-steel-production-and-2024-global-totals/

Defence Budget by Country (2025) https://www.globalfirepower.com/defense-spending-budget.php#google_vignette

Disha Ray, Social Political and Economic Landscape in Kautilya's *Arthashastra*, 04 June 2020, https://www.worldhistory.org/article/

1561/social-political—economic-landscapes-in-kautilyas/

Gary Hamel, C K Prahalad, *Competing for the Future*, McGraw Hill Education Private Limited, 2014, ISBN 9780040486713

Global Ship Building Race of 2025, https://www.shipuniverse.com/global-shipbuilding-race-of-2025/

https://archive.nytimes.com/www.nytimes.com/fodors/top/features/travel/destinations/centralandsouthamerica/brazil/riodejaneiro/fdrs_feat_129_9.html

https://data.worldbank.org/indicator/GB.XPD.RSDV.GD.ZS?locations=CN

https://knoema.com/mhrzolg/historical-gdp-by-country-statistics-from-the-world-bank-1960-2019

https://thegedi.org/global-entrepreneurship-and-development-index/

https://thegedi.org/global-entrepreneurship-and-development-index/

https://time.com/collection/worlds-best-companies-2024/

https://www.britannica.com/place/Brazil/Ongoing-domestic-migration

https://www.britannica.com/topic/history-of-Russia

https://www.ducksters.com/geography/country/russia_history_timeline.php

https://www.forbes.com/lists/global2000/

https://www.oecd.org/cfe/leed/Entrepreneurial-ecosystems.pdf Entrepreneurial eco system and growth oriented entrepreneurship

https://www.statista.com/statistics/1113045/fastest-growing-companies-brazil/

https://www.vifindia.org/article/2025/may/28/Op-Sindoor-Is-India-Moving-Towards-Unified-Theatre-Command

Kangle RP, *The Kautilya Arthasastra*, Part 2, Published by Motilal Banarsidass, New Delhi, 1972, ISBN 81-208-0040-0

Kissinger Henry, *World Order*, Penguin Books, 2015, ISBN 9780143127710

KPMG Top Global Risks, 2025, https://kpmg.com/xx/en/our-insights/risk-and-regulation/top-risks-forecast-2025.html

Ministry of MSMEs, 'The Contribution of MSMEs to the GDP (22 July 2024), https://www.pib.gov.in/PressReleaseIframePage.aspx?PRID=2035073

PwC Corporate Income Tax Rates by Country (2025), https://taxsummaries.pwc.com/quick-charts/corporate-income-tax-cit-rates

PwC GDPs of Countries 1960-2019, https://knoema.com/mhrzolg/historical-gdp-by-country-statistics-from-the-world-bank-1960-2019

Rangarajan L N, *Kautilya: The Arthashastra*, Penguin Books New Delhi, 1990, ISBN 9780140446036

Roger L. Martin & Sally Osberg, "Social Entrepreneurship The Case for Definition," Spring 2007

Shamasastry R, *Kautilya's Arthasastra*, Fifth Edition 1956, Raghubir Printing Press, Mysore, India

Sharma Ruchir, *Breakout Nations In Pursuit of Next Economic Miracles*, Penguin Books, 2012, ISBN 9780241957813

SS Khanaka, *Entrepreneurial Development National Institute of Financial Management, Ministry of Finance Government of India*, S Chand and Company Limited, New Delhi, 2008, ISBN 9788121918015

Statistics Times (2019), "Comparing China and India by Economy", http://statisticstimes.com/economy/china-vs-india-economy.php, Accessed on 5 August 2020. 23 Ashok Pathak (2020), India's Strategies for Information War and Cyber Deterrence, New Delhi

The Hindu, 21 March 2023, Top 22% Firms remit 90% to GST Kitty, (https://www.thehindu.com/business/Economy/top-22-firms-remit-90-of-gst-kitty-says-union-finance-minister-nirmala-sitharaman/article66645644.ece

The World's Real Time Billionaires (2025), https://www.forbes.com/real-time-billionaires/#6509b3a13d78

Top Companies in India by Market Capitalisation (2025), https://www.moneycontrol.com/stocks/marketinfo/marketcap/bse/textiles-apparel.html

UNESCO (n.d.), "How Much Does Your Country Invest in R&D?", UNESCO Institute for Statistics, http://uis.unesco.org/apps/visualisations/research-and-development-spending/, Accessed on 25 July 2020.

Veronique Bouchard and Alian Fayolle, *Corporate Entrepreneurship*, Routledge Taylor and Francis Group, London and New York, ISBN 978113881368

What an entrepreneurship ecosystem actually is https://hbr.org/2014/05/what-an-entrepreneurial-ecosystem-actually-is by Daniel Isenberg (HBR 2014).

Chapter Three: Military Power

AFI (22 March 2025), Indian Army T90 tanks set for a surprise power boost with 1350 HP engine upgrade, https://idrw.org/indian-armys-t-90-tanks-set-for-a-surprise-power-boost-with-1350-hp-engine-upgrade/

Behera Laxman Kumar, *Indian Defense Industry: An Agenda for Making in India*, Institute of Defense Studies and Analysis (New Delhi), Pentagon Press, 2016. ISBN 978-81-8274-905-4.

CII Micro Medium and Small Scale Industries, https://www.cii.in/Sectors.aspx?enc=prvePUj2bdMtgTmvPwvisYH+5EnGjyGXO9hLECvTuNuXK6QP3tp4gPGuPr/xpT2f

Commercial aircraft market size, https://www.alliedmarketresearch.com/commercial-aircraft-market#:~:text=The%20global%20commercial%20aircraft%20market,5.3%25%20from%202024%20to%202033

Dassault Aviation 'From Ouragan to Rafale', https://www.dassault-aviation.com/en/passion/from-ouragan-to-rafale/from-ouragan-to-rafale/

Defence Market Size Share Growth and Trend Overview Business Research Insight (March 2025), https://www.businessresearchinsights.com/market-reports/defence-market-109136#:~:text=The%20global%20defence%20market%20size,period%20from%202025%20to%202033.

Deshpande Rohit, Raina Anjali (December 2011), The Ordinary Heroes of the Taj, https://hbr.org/2011/12/the-ordinary-heroes-of-the-taj#:~:text=Summary.&text=When%20terrorists%20attacked%20the%20Indian,cases%2C%20 sacrificing %E2%80%94their%20lives, accessed on 15 May 2024

Grant Robert (CMR 1991), The Resource Baaed Theory of Competitive Advantage: Implications for Strategy Formulation, https://ocw.mit.edu/courses/15-902-strategic-management-i-fall-2006/ec11443248418460e5d18a9b03c4bde0_rbv_theoryf_ca.pdf accessed on 18 May 18, 2024.

Hill John (2024), 'India Orders 240 engines for Su30MKI Fighter Fleet', https://www.airforce-technology.com/news/india-orders-240-engines-for-su-30-mki-fighter-fleet/#:~:text=The%20Su%2D30MKI%20is%20powered,of%20300%20metres%20per%20second

https://companiesmarketcap.com/china/largest-companies-in-china-by-market-cap/#google_vignette

https://growthbug.com/indias-100-unicorns-ranked-by-revenue-losses-current-valuation-revenue-multiple-5c2c92ae0b38

https://msme.gov.in/sites/default/files/FINALMSMEANNUALREPORT2023-24ENGLISH.pdf

https://timesofindia.indiatimes.com/education/news/the-great-indian-employment-paradox-the-more-you-learn-the-less-you-earn/articleshow/113627394.cms

https://www.bseindia.com/markets/equity/eqreports/topmarketcapitalization.aspx

https://www.business-standard.com/economy/news/young-indians-more-likely-to-be-jobless-if-they-are-educated-ilo-data-124032900038_1.html

https://www.thehindu.com/opinion/op-ed/are-indian-startups-not-scaling-up-on-innovation/article69462055.ece

IAF set to showcase LCA Tejas Mk1 on Global stage

India Defence Market Report by Type and Region 2025-2033, IMAC Report, https://www.imarcgroup.com/india-defense-market#:~:text=Market%20Overview%3A,5.76%25%20during%202025%2D2033

India's Top 100 Billionaires, https://www.fortuneindia.com

Institute for Competitiveness, NITI Aayog Enhancing MSMEs Competitiveness, https://www.niti.gov.in/sites/default/files/2025-05/Enhancing_Competitiveness_of_MSMEs_in_India.pdf

Military Aircraft Market Size and Trends, https://www.coherentmarketinsights.com/market-insight/military-aircraft-market-5311#:~:text=Global %20military%20aircraft%20market%20is,4.8%25%20from%202025%20to%202032.

Ovidijus Jurevicius (October 2023), Resource Based View accessed from https://strategicmanagementinsight.com/tools/resource-based-view/ accessed on 18 May 2024.

Pathak Ashok (19 Sep 2022), Indigenisation of Defence Production from Vision to Outcome, https://www.vifindia.org/article/2022/september/19/indigenization-of-defence-production

Pathak Ashok, https://www.vifindia.org/article/2025/may/09/Indigenization-of-Indian-Air-Force-Strategic-Shift-in-Political-Economy

Performance Audit on 'Design, Development, Manufacture Induction of LCA', https://cag.gov.in/uploads/download_audit_report/2015/Union_Performance_Defense_Design__Manufacture_Light_Combat%20Aircraft_17_2015_chapter_5.pdf

Rangarajan L N, *Kautilya: The Arthashastra*, Penguin Books, Random House India ISBN 9780140446036

Rohit Deshpande and Anjali Raina, *HBR Magazine*, Ordinary Heroes of the Taj (2011) https://hbr.org/2011/12/the-ordinary-heroes-of-the-taj

Shyamlesh Kumar Tiwari, G P Shastri, Chaukhamba Surbharti Prakashan Varanasi, 2020, ISBN 9789386554000, Daryaganj New Delh

Singh Suresh (Air Vice Marshal), Aeroengine Fundamentals and Landscape in India A Way Forward (Centre for Air Power Studies), KW Publishers, 2024, ISBN 9788196585020

Tejas Mark (Mk) 1 Light Combat Supersonic Fighter India (Air Force Technology 19 July 2024), https://www.airforce-technology.com/projects/tejas/?cf-view

Chapter Four: Geopolitics

Dudney Daniel H, Britannica Political Science Geopolitics, https://www.britannica.com/topic/geopolitics

Equality Figures, World Bank, https://www.pib.gov.in/PressNoteDetails.aspx?NoteId=154837&ModuleId=3

Flint Collin (07 July 2024), Everyone is talking About Geopolitics what is geopolitics, https://www.e-ir.info/2024/07/07/everyone-is-talking-about-it-but-what-is-geopolitics/

Geetanath V, Hyderabad Firm Develops Drone Defence Dome, *The Hindu* (9 July 2021), https://www.thehindu.com/news/cities/Hyderabad/hyderabad-firm-develops-drone-defence-dome/article35227828.ece

Government of India, Press Information Bureau, 2025, S&P Improves India's Sovereign Rating to BBB, https://www.pib.gov.in/PressNoteDetails.

aspx?NoteId=1 55041&ModuleId=3#:~:text=S%26P%20Global%20has %20raised%20India's,funda mentals%20and%20prudent%20policy %20management.

https://www.weforum.org/stories/2024/11/brics-summit-geopolitics-bloc-international/

India-US Trade, IBEF, Feb 2025, https://www.ibef.org/indian-exports/india-us-trade

International Banker (2023), Indian Rupee as International Currency, https://internationalbanker.com/banking/the-indian-rupee-as-international-currency/#:~:text=The%20Indian%20rupee%20is%20accepted,tender %20in%20Nepal%20and%20Bhutan.

Ministry of Tourism, Press Release, 19 December 2024, India's Ranking in Travel and Tourism, https://www.pib.gov.in/PressReleasePage.aspx?PRID=2086019

S&P Global Top Geopolitical Risks of 2025, https://www.spglobal.com/en/research-insights/market-insights/geopolitical-risk

WEF Ranking, 2025, https://www3.weforum.org/docs/GCR2017-2018/03CountryProfiles/Standalone2-pagerprofiles/WEF_GCI_2017_2018_Profile_India.pdf

Appendices

Highlights of Prime Minister's Speech 15 August 2025*

The Prime Minister Shri Narendra Modi addressed the Nation on the 79th Independence Day from the ramparts of the Red Fort, Delhi today. The address to the nation by Shri Modi was the longest and most decisive address from the Red Fort, lasting 103 minutes, charting a bold roadmap for a Viksit Bharat by 2047. Prime Minister's address focussed on self-reliance, innovation, and citizen empowerment, highlighting India's journey from a nation dependent on others to a globally confident, technologically advanced, and economically resilient country.

Shri Modi outlined the vision for a Viksit Bharat 2047, emphasising that India's progress is built on self-reliance, innovation, and citizen empowerment. He stated that across sectors ranging from strategic defence to semiconductors, clean energy to agriculture, and digital sovereignty to youth empowerment, the roadmap seeks to transform India into a $10 trillion economy by 2047, making it globally competitive, socially inclusive, and strategically autonomous.

**Source:* https://www.pmindia.gov.in/en/news_updates/highlights-from-the-pms-address-on-the-79th-independence-day/

Following are the highlights from the Prime Minister's address.

1. General

- This grand festival of Independence is a celebration of the 140 crore resolutions of our people.
- India is continuously strengthening the spirit of unity.
- For 75 years, the Constitution of Bharat has been guiding us like a lighthouse.
- Dr. Syama Prasad Mookerjee was the first great personality of the nation to sacrifice his life for the Constitution of Bharat.
- Nature is testing us all. In the past few days, we have faced many natural disasters—landslides, cloudbursts, and countless other calamities.
- Today serves as a great opportunity to salute the brave warriors of Operation SINDOOR from the ramparts of the Red Fort.
- Bharat has now decided that we will no longer tolerate the nuclear threats which has been endured so long.
- If our enemies continue the acts of terrorism in the future, our army will decide on its own terms, at the time of its choosing, in the manner it deems fit, and target the objectives it selects and we will act accordingly. We will give a fitting and crushing response.
- India has now decided, blood and water will not flow together. The people have realised that the Indus Waters Treaty was unjust. Water from the Indus River system irrigated enemy lands while our farmers suffered.
- The Indus water treaty is unacceptable to us in the interest of our farmers, and in the interest of the nation.
- The bedrock of a Viksit Bharat is also a self-reliant Bharat.
- It is a great Misfortune when dependency becomes a habit

and when we do not even realise and abandon self-reliance and become dependent on others.

- Self-reliance is linked to our capability, and when self-reliance begins to diminish, our capability too continually declines. Therefore, to preserve, maintain, and enhance our capability, it is imperative to be self-reliant.
- India is today creating a modern ecosystem in every sector and the modern ecosystem will make our country self-reliant in every field.
- "I call upon the youth of the nation to bring forward their innovative ideas. Today's idea could shape the future of generations to come. I will stand shoulder to shoulder with you in this journey", said Shri Modi.
- Drawing inspiration from India's COVID-19 response, where indigenous vaccines and platforms like CoWin saved millions of lives globally, we must expand this spirit of innovation.
- Our scientists and youth should build our own jet engines taking it up as a direct challenge.
- Researchers and entrepreneurs must secure patents for new drugs and medical technologies, ensuring that India not only meets its own healthcare needs but also becomes a global hub of medical self-reliance and innovation, demonstrating the country's ability to lead in science, technology, and human welfare.
- The National Manufacturing Mission is progressing at great speed.
- A large share of India's budget still goes toward importing petrol, diesel, and gas. The **National Deepwater Exploration Mission** will be launched to harness India's offshore energy resources, boosting energy self-reliance and reducing dependence on foreign fuel imports, marking another step toward a fully independent and powerful India.

- Citizens and shopkeepers should champion India-made goods under the "Vocal for Local" initiative.
- Swadeshi should stem from pride and strength, not compulsion.
- We must push for visible promotion, such as "Swadeshi" boards outside shops, to boost self-reliance, support entrepreneurship, and strengthen India's economic and industrial base.
- India's strength lies in its people, innovation, and commitment to self-reliance.
- Over the past decade, India has been reforming, performing, and transforming, but now the time has come to move forward with even greater strength.
- Our government is committed to creating a modern, efficient, and citizen-friendly ecosystem, where laws, regulations, and processes are simplified, entrepreneurship is encouraged, and every Indian can contribute to building a Viksit Bharat.
- A **Task Force for Next-Generation Reforms** will be formed, which will evaluate all current laws, rules, and procedures related to economic activities. The Task Force will work within a set timeline to:
  - Reduce compliance costs for startups, MSMEs, and entrepreneurs
  - Provide freedom from fear of arbitrary legal actions
  - Ensure laws are streamlined for ease of doing business

  These reforms are aimed at creating a supportive ecosystem for innovation, entrepreneurship, and economic growth.
- We are working with a saturation approach to ensure social justice.
- Today, the government comes to your doorstep with a saturation approach. Crores of beneficiaries are receiving

the benefits of government schemes, and Direct Benefit Transfer has been a truly revolutionary step.

- Today, over 25 crore poor people in the last 10 years — have overcome poverty and stepped out of it, creating a new "neo–middle class."
- We are not concerned only with socially backward groups, we also want to give priority to backward regions though aspirational districts and blocks programmes.
- India will no longer compromise on its national interests, and the operation underscored the country's ability to act swiftly and decisively, relying entirely on indigenous technology and defence platforms.
- Dependence on others raises questions about a nation's independence. It is unfortunate when dependence becomes a habit, a dangerous one. That's why we must remain aware and committed to becoming self-reliant. Self-reliance is not just about exports, imports, the rupee, or the dollar. It is about our capabilities, our strength to stand on our own.
- Reform is not just about economics, it is about transforming the everyday lives of citizens.
- The reforms undertaken by our Government signal a modern, citizen-centric government where ordinary people can experience ease, fairness, and empowerment.
- India is committed to structural, regulatory, policy, process, and procedural reforms, building a nation where governance works for the people, not the other way around.
- Instead of focusing on others' limitations, India must extend its own line of progress.
- In a world of rising economic self-interest, the focus must be on strengthening India's capabilities, expanding opportunities, and empowering citizens. These reforms mark the beginning of an accelerated phase of governance

transformation, ensuring India is more resilient, inclusive, and globally competitive.

- Every Indian must contribute to nation-building, whether by buying India-made products or participating in scientific, technological, and entrepreneurial ventures to ensure a prosperous, powerful, and Viksit Bharat by the nation's centenary of independence.
- To build a developed India, we will neither stop nor bow down, we will keep working hard and we will build a developed India before our eyes in 2047.
- We will not allow even a single particle of slavery to remain in our lives, in our systems, in our rules, laws and traditions. We will not rest until we are free from all forms of slavery.
- We will be proud of our heritage. The biggest ornament, the biggest jewel, the biggest crown jewel of our identity is our heritage, we will be proud of our heritage.
- Unity is the most powerful mantra among all these and hence it will be our collective resolve that no one should be able to break the thread of unity.

2. Ministry of Defence

- Operation SINDOOR is a demonstration of India's defence self-reliance and our strategic autonomy.
- The results of our consistent mission over the past ten years towards self-reliance in the field of defence was shown in Operation SINDOOR.
- Using Made-in-India weapons, the operation dismantled terror networks and Pakistan-based infrastructure, signalling a new era where India will no longer accept nuclear blackmail or threats on foreign terms.
- The indigenous capabilities, including Made-in-India weapons, enable India to act decisively and independently, proving that national security cannot rely on foreign dependence.

- Indian innovators and youth should develop jet engines within India, ensuring that future defence technology is entirely home-grown and self-reliant.
- India draws inspiration from its rich cultural and mythological heritage to guide modern defence innovations. To strengthen **India's offensive and deterrent capabilities,** we are launching **"Mission Sudarshan Chakra",** aimed at neutralising enemy defence infiltrations and enhancing India's offensive capabilities.
- Akin to the legendary Shri Krishna's Sudarshan Chakra, this mission underscores India's commitment to strategic autonomy, ensuring rapid, precise, and powerful responses to any threat.
- The initiative is designed to enhance rapid, precise, and powerful defence responses, reinforcing India's strategic autonomy.
- All public places will be covered by an expanded nationwide security shield by 2035, ensuring comprehensive protection for the nation while showcasing India's commitment to self-reliant defence.

3. Ministry of Finance

- Next-Generation GST reforms by Diwali will reduce taxes on daily essentials, benefiting MSMEs, local vendors, and consumers, while simultaneously stimulating economic growth and creating a more efficient, citizen-friendly economy.
- Income Tax Reform and Faceless Assessment were introduced making the tax system transparent and efficient.
- Exempting income up to ₹ 12 lakh from income tax has brought great joy to my middle-class families, who are eager to contribute to nation-building.

- For the world to recognise our strength in manufacturing, we must constantly scale new heights in quality by adhering to Zero Defect, Zero Effect products.
- Every product of ours should have higher value, but cost less. It is with this spirit that we must move forward.
- Amidst global instability, India's fiscal discipline, the energy of India's finance, remains a ray of hope, with the entire world expressing confidence in the Indian economy.

4. Ministry of Home Affairs

- It is of prime importance to safeguard India's demographic integrity.
- The imminent dangers of demographic imbalance due to infiltration and illegal migration in border areas is high, thereby affecting citizens' livelihoods.
- A **High-Powered Demography Mission** will be launched aimed at ensuring India's unity, integrity, and security, tackling both strategic and social challenges.
- Our tribal areas and youth were caught in the clutches of Maoism. Today, we have reduced that number from over 125 districts to merely 20.
- Regions once known as the "Red Corridor" are now becoming corridors of green development. This is a matter of pride for us.
- In those parts of Bharat's map once stained red with blood, we have now hoisted the tricolour of the Constitution, the rule of law, and development.

5. Ministry of Agriculture & Farmers' Welfare

- India's farmers are the backbone of the nation's journey from dependency to self-reliance.
- The colonial rule had left the country impoverished, but it was the tireless efforts of farmers that filled Bharat's granaries and secured the nation's food sovereignty.

- India will not compromise on its farmers' interests.
- "I have stood as a wall for the farmers and livestock keepers against any detrimental policy, protecting their rights and livelihoods", stated the Prime Minister.
- Last year, Indian Farmers broke all previous records in the production of grains.
- Agriculture remains a cornerstone of India's development, with India No. 1 in milk, pulses, and jute, and No. 2 in rice, wheat, cotton, fruits, and vegetables.
- Agricultural exports have crossed ₹ 4 lakh crore, reflecting the nation's global competitiveness.
- To further empower farmers, the Pradhan Mantri Dhan-Dhanya Krishi Yojana was launched for 100 backward farming districts, complementing ongoing support through PM-Kisan, irrigation schemes, and livestock protection programs, ensuring that India's backbone of prosperity remains strong and resilient.
- Government schemes such as PM Kisan Samman Nidhi, rainwater harvesting, irrigation projects, quality seed distribution, and timely fertiliser supply have together boosted farmers' confidence across the country.

6. Ministry of Animal Husbandry

In North India alone, around 125 crore free doses of vaccinations have been administered to cattle to prevent Foot and Mouth disease.

7. Ministry of Electronics & Information Technology

- Attempts to set up semiconductor factories 50–60 years ago were "killed at birth" while other nations prospered, India is now on mission mode in semiconductor manufacturing.
- India will launch Made in India semiconductor chips by the end of 2025, reflecting the nation's growing strength in critical technology sectors

- Innovation in AI, cyber security, deep-tech, and operating systems is necessary for global competitiveness.

8. Department of Space

- The whole of India rejoices in the remarkable achievements of Group Captain Shubhanshu Shukla.
- India is preparing for Aatmanirbhar Bharat Gaganyaan, with ambitious plans for India's very own space station, signalling a new era of indigenous space capabilities.
- Over 300 startups are actively innovating in satellites, exploration, and cutting-edge space technologies, ensuring that India is not just participating but leading globally in space science and exploration.

9. Department of Atomic Energy

- 10 new nuclear reactors are currently operational and by India's 100th year of independence, the nation aims to increase its nuclear energy capacity tenfold, strengthening energy self-reliance and supporting sustainable growth.
- India is opening the nuclear sector to private players, creating unprecedented opportunities in energy and technology.
- If India were not dependent on energy imports, the money saved could be used for the welfare of farmers, further strengthening the backbone of the nation's prosperity.

10. Ministry of Labour and Employment

- A major employment scheme – PM Viksit Bharat Rozgar Yojana, worth ₹ 1 lakh crore will be launched. Under the scheme, newly employed youth will receive ₹ 15,000. The scheme aims to benefit 3 crore young Indians, strengthening the bridge from Swatantra Bharat to Samriddha Bharat.
- This initiative will transform India's demographic potential into real economic and social prosperity,

strengthening the bridge from Swatantra Bharat to Samriddha Bharat and empowering the youth to actively contribute to the nation's progress and development.

11. Ministry of Micro, Small and Medium Enterprises

- Next-generation GST reforms will be unveiled on Diwali, reducing taxes on essential goods and providing relief to MSMEs, local vendors, and consumers.
- The government's reforms aim to reduce compliance costs for startups, MSMEs, and entrepreneurs, while ensuring freedom from the fear of outdated legal provisions. This creates a more conducive environment for business growth, encouraging innovation and economic self-reliance.

12. Ministry of Chemicals and Fertilisers

- India should strengthen itself as the "pharmacy of the world".
- There is an urgent need to invest more in research and development.
- "Shouldn't we be the ones providing the best and most affordable medicines for the welfare of humanity?"
- India's growing strength in domestic pharmaceutical innovation, emphasising the need to develop new medicines, vaccines, and life-saving treatments entirely within India.
- Food security cannot be left vulnerable to imports.
- There is an urgent need for domestic production of fertilisers and key inputs, ensuring that Indian farmers are empowered and that Bharat's agriculture thrives independently.
- We must find new ways to manufacture our own fertilisers as per the requirement of India, without depending on other countries.

- This is critical not only for farmers' welfare but also for strengthening the nation's economic sovereignty.

13. Ministry of Women & Child Development

- The women's self-help groups have done wonders, with their products reaching global markets across the world.
- India's daughters are dominating from startups to the space sector, from sports to the armed forces. They are proudly participating in the country's development journey by standing shoulder to shoulder.
- Namo Drone Didi Nari Shakti became a new identity for women.
- We pledge to make three crore women 'Lakhpati Didis'.

14. Ministry of Law & Justice

- Over the past years, the government has undertaken a historic wave of reforms, abolishing over 40,000 unnecessary compliances and repealing more than 1,500 outdated laws.
- Dozens of other laws were simplified in Parliament, always keeping citizens' interests at the forefront.
- In the recent session alone, over 280 provisions were removed, making governance simpler and more accessible for every Indian.
- We have abolished the penal code and brought in Bharatiya Nyay Sanhita, embodying trust in the citizens of Bharat, a sense of belonging, and filled with sensitivity.

15. Ministry of Health and Family Welfare

- Obesity is becoming a very grave crisis for our nation.
- Every family should resolve to use 10 percent less cooking oil to fight obesity.

16. Ministry of Tribal Affairs

- Today, after being freed from Maoism and Naxalism, Bastar's youth participate in the Olympics.
- This year marks the 150th birth anniversary of Bhagwan Birsa Munda. By freeing these tribal areas from Naxalism and saving the lives of the youth of my tribal families, we have paid him a true tribute.

17. Ministry of Culture

- This year marks the 350th martyrdom anniversary of Guru Tegh Bahadur Ji, who sacrificed everything for the protection of our culture and values.
- The strength of our culture lies in our diversity.
- The success of the 'Maha Kumbh' is a resounding testament to Bharat's unity and strength.
- We have accorded classical language status to Marathi, Assamese, Bangla, Pali, and Prakrit.
- The more our languages develop, the more enriched they become, the stronger our entire knowledge system will grow.
- Under the Gyan Bharatam Mission, we are now working across the nation to locate handwritten texts, manuscripts, and centuries-old documents, and to use today's technology to preserve their wealth of knowledge for future generations.
- I salute all the Swayamsevaks who have contributed to this century-long journey of national service, and the nation takes pride in this grand and dedicated journey of 100 years of the Rashtriya Swayamsevak Sangh, which will continue to inspire us.

18. Ministry of New and Renewable Energy

- Energy independence is of prime importance for the bright future of youth and for welfare of farmers and this will be done.

- With our resolve of Self-reliance in energy in the last 11 years, solar energy in India has seen a thirtyfold increase.
- With Mission Green Hydrogen, Bharat is today investing thousands of crores of rupees
- While the world debates global warming, India had resolved to achieve 50 percent clean energy by 2030 yet, thanks to the commitment of its people, that goal was met by 2025.
- Solar, nuclear, hydro, and hydrogen energy have been advanced, marking a decisive step towards energy independence.

19. Ministry of Power

- Be it solar panels or components required for electric vehicles, we should manufacture our own components.

20. Ministry of Mines

- To secure resources essential for energy, industry, and defence, India has launched the **National Critical Minerals Mission**, exploring 1,200 sites to ensure access to minerals essential for energy, industry, and defence.
- Controlling these minerals strengthens strategic autonomy, ensuring India's industrial and defence sectors remain self-reliant.

21. Ministry of Youth Affairs & Sports

- The youth must develop India's own social media platforms and digital infrastructure, ensuring communication, data, and technological ecosystems remain secure and independent, reinforcing India's digital autonomy.
- To promote sports, we have brought forth the National Sports Policy.
- We have introduced the 'Khelo India Policy' in the country.

Note: Some items have involvement of more than one ministry, accordingly they may be repeated.

An Analysis : Initiatives Taken, Progress Made and the Larger Scope Derived from the Prime Minister's Speech

The speech has a very clear indication to trajectory for Vision 2047. It covers the achievements, concerns and the road to the destination – 2047 and beyond. While speaking on infrastructure development in the capital, garbage menace, cleaning of River Yamuna, slums and linking languages to the ancient culture the massage is on urbanisation, urban development and reviving the rich cultural heritage. This includes citizen centric economic development. These can be linked to all the digital platforms (education, health, citizen connect, governance, environment) mentioned in Arvind Virmani's paper on Viksit Bharat.

A World Bank Report on urbanisation in India brings out huge opportunities and cautions of serious challenges. By 2050, the report forecasts India's urban population to be 951 million. 144 million new houses will be required. Urban India has the capability to contribute much higher percentage to the national GDP. It will require about US $ 2.4 trillion investment for improvement in infrastructure. Climatic changes, floods and waste management are major challenges in Indian urban centers. At present the urban infrastructure – primarily to safeguard the citizens from waste, heat and flooding is unsatisfactory. It made the Chief Justice of India to remark that two hours of rain can bring the national capital to a grinding halt. The other metros like Mumbai, Bengluru, Chennai etc. are no better. It is not that the present government has suddenly started thinking of urban development. In-fact the efforts to improve Indian cities commenced more than six years back. The smart city initiative created several clean and 'good to live in' cities like Bhubaneshwar, Indore, Pune, Ahmedabad, Surat etc. Similar initiatives were taken around the same time for creating ideal villages. Thus, the work is in progress. Guidelines are in place.

Healthy competition has been generated. What is required now are more commitment and acceleration. Thus, here is a huge opportunity and equally huge challenge. India has a critical opportunity to drive resilient urban development, says new World Bank report (22 July 2025)

While speaking on swadeshi he spoke about charkha, khadi revolution, vocal for local slogan. It is direct reference to globally relevant self-reliance. He did speak on the MSMEs, quality, cost and zero defect. This includes motivation as also caution. Self-reliance will be a non-starter if the Indian goods and services are poor in quality and high on cost. The Japanese do not buy the Japanese cars because these are Japanese. The Japanese cars are bought world over including the US citizens in Detroit because these cars are considered better and give value for money. The same would be true for Indian goods and services. It is human nature to buy the best (in terms of customer defined quality) at the lowest cost. There was a time when Indians were known to use dubious means to buy foreign goods and services. Post liberalisation this has stopped since those foreign goods are available in India at much lesser price (import duty reduction). Indian goods will replace foreign goods purchased by Indians if the Indian goods are better. This is what is implied by the Prime Minister when he said high quality and low cost. Interestingly made in India cars by Suzuki-Maruti are being bought by the Japanese since they find these cars giving better quality at lower costs.

A less known fact among the business houses is that quality does not add to cost. On the contrary quality has no cost. A Six Sigma process driven quality approach cuts down costs by many orders. The Japanese control the quality at the input and process levels. A lean manufacturing and six sigma approach. The West (including India) apply quality check at the output level. There is a huge difference between the two. Gary Hamel (Competing for the Future) stated in his book that Japanese are able to manufacture a brand – new Lexus luxury car in the cost that Mercedes spend on output-based quality control of one Mercedes car of similar standard. As per opinion survey the Indian customers perceive international product to be of better quality. The Indian retailers assume that this skewness is due to lack of marketing. Well, this is partially true. The sale of Khadi products increased seven folds due to better quality, customer satisfaction and then marketing.

The Deccan Herald report on quality of Indian manufactured goods paints a dismal picture when it comes to quality-based attractiveness of Indian goods. Though India ranks sixth in the world in terms of volume of manufactured goods our ranking in terms of export (that is based on competition in quality and cost) is at 17th, below Switzerland and Taiwan. On the other hand, the quality of Indian services is considered much higher. This appears to be a major concern that Prime Minister had when he exhorted zero defect and low cost. Incidentally the Six Sigma standards are 3.42 defects per million – as good as zero.

Why is our quality low and cost not so competitive? The answer lies in subsidies, pro small bias, wealth creation is considered a crime and lack of national perspective in starting a business enterprise. There is a very high percentage of entrepreneurs who enter commercial activities for making money – quick money and lots of it. This is reflected in our tendency to remain small, not investing in R&D, focus on avoiding taxation and constantly asking for government support. We have discussed this earlier. The Prime Minister emphasised this in his own way.

Security was another critical issue the Prime Minister included in his address. The first and generally overlooked factor, related to security was menace of illegal migrants. The independence of India was accompanied by one of the most tragic event of partition – people massacred in millions and suffered worse human miseries. A large number of Muslims in undivided India first moved to Pakistan – their new home. They soon returned to India when they found that the picture there was not so bright. A vast majority of Hindus migrated to India and never returned to their erstwhile homes in Pakistan. Citizenship of India became a complex issue further muddied by political naivety.

In Punjab the citizenship was decided through a combination of religious affinity and permit system. Partition of Bengal created a bigger problem. The migration of people from the erstwhile East Pakistan continued between 1971 to 1991 and 1991 to 2014. In 2001 about one-third of the Assamese population (33.8 millions) consisted of these immigrants. Bulk of these immigrants are Muslims. From 1971 to 2001 the Muslim population in this part of India increased from one million to around 1.7 million. The Hindu migrant population increased from 3.5 million to 8.2 million. Most of these are illegal entrants into India. Overall the estimate of illegal Muslim migrants to India range from 2.3 million to 20 million. Besides the North East there are large number of illegal Muslim immigrants in Maharashtra (especially Mumbai) and Rajasthan. In addition, forty thousand Rohingya Muslims too have migrated to India from Myanmar. The Government of India has firmly rejected the proposal to grant citizenship to the Rohingya Muslims.

The illegal Muslim migrants to India are not like any other such migrants in rest of the world. The bitterness of partition persists. Theology based sub national feeling add another dimension to national security – making India a fertile ground for the Deep State within and outside India. This threat to the nation from the Deep State coupled with woke needs to be seen as part of cyber threat. Narrative building and misinformation have become very effective tools for launching perception and net war through the cyber space with the help of Artificial Intelligence.

Vulnerability of India's Cyber Space

During his presentation at Vigyan Bhawan on 29 October 2018, Dr Saraswat traced the growth of cyber threats in terms of number and types. There has been an exponential growth in cyber threats since 2005. This was not only in terms of number of attacks but the likely damage these attacks would cause. Thus, insertion of Trojan Horses and worms (which could be activated later) started and increased very rapidly since 2008. Saraswat also informed that from 2012 onwards phishing and identity threats increased. Cyber espionage and cyber war related attacks (computer network exploitation) increased since 2010. The attacks pertaining to Denial of Service (DoS) and Distributed Denial of Service (DDoS) increased since 2016. The advanced cyber weapons' threats increased post 2017.

An analysis by Data Security Council of India (DSCI) has reported unprecedented increase in the number and sophistication of cyber threats to India in 2025. More than eight million digital platforms were targeted with 369 million cyber attacks. The top most target was Banking and Financial Services Institutes (BFSI), health care and hospitality.

In terms of inherent vulnerabilities of cyberspace emanating from the way Internet came to the present shape, following aspects are noteworthy to plan comprehensive measures to fix the threats:

- **Evolution and structure of Internet:** When Internet opened up from defence and academic use to society at large, accessibility and interoperability became the key requirements. Hence, the entire architecture was hinged on easiest access, lack of identification, authentication, repudiation, and ethics.
- **Proliferation of mobile network:** As the mobile spectrum moved from 3G to 5G distinction between

mobile and fixed line internet disappeared. Add to this the exponential growth of the social media, which is least regulated and which also hates regulation of any kind; the vulnerability of cyberspace multiplied manifold. The type of people who use smart phones are not keen or capable of understanding the security issues.

- **Internet of things:** With growing clamour for online operations, control, and repairs, the Internet extended to every single appliance, platform, system that could be handled through the software. This included almost everything that we use in our daily life or for war-fighting. By automating the Supervisory Control and Data Acquisition (SCADA), the threat spectrum moved from disruptive to destructive zone.
- **Emergence of supply chain management (SCM) concepts in manufacturing of hardware:** In order to enhance the potency and capability of the systems, computer hardware as also all other products and services are being provided through managing supply chains involving a very large number of independent enterprises spread over many countries in several continents. These enterprises are bound together by financial and inter-SCM competitions. Thus during military conflicts the national loyalties overtake business ethics. The manufacturers may leave trapdoors in the hardware to be used later. Alternatively, they can share the hardware vulnerability with unauthorised agencies or persons.
- **Software design:** The unintentional discrepancies as well as those introduced by the software designer to be used later are exploited for attacking the network.

Cyber Security

While building up appropriate infrastructure and culture for information security at the national level, we also need to consider creating defensive and offensive capabilities in the cyber war domain for the Armed Forces. The VIF Task Force Report on Credible Cyber Deterrence gives out detailed modalities for the purpose. Specific aspects related to identifying skill sets and career progression of personnel in this organisation are given below:

- **Cyber literate:** Basic aspects of cyber security to be practised by all those who use a device or system (Operators' skills).
- **Cyber operator:** Cleaning of devices, systems and networks of malware, virus. Inserting security patches, social media monitoring, website security and unit level cyber security audit.
- **Cyber warrior:** Maintain cyberspace information of select adversaries/targets, prepare operating systems on open source languages such as Linux, identify resources for crowdsourcing of cyber operation if required etc. IITs, Forensic Science University Gujarat, JNU (for psychology and behavioural economy).
- **Cyber leader:** Cyber expert on big data, machine learning, AI, psychology, psychology forensic. These leaders need to be trained by premier academic institutes with active involvement of concerned government organisations tasked for the role.
- **Coordinators in National Cyber Security Board:** Some of the select think-tank organisations need to be dedicated for this purpose.

War Against Terrorism

The war against terrorism commenced soon after independence. Earlier its intensity was much more in the North East – a China sponsored insurgency. Since 1989 the intensity shifted to the J&K. However, during the last eleven years India has been consistently winning this war through a tough politico military action. Naxal insurgency has been controlled to a large extent. Reduction of insurgency in J&K presents an interesting picture if we see the statistics over three time periods.

War Against Terrorism from 1989 to 10 May 2025

Period	*SF Martyred (average per year)*	*Terrorists killed (average per year)*	*Civilian casualties (average per year)*
1989–2016	6273 (224)	23132 (826)	14738 (508)
2017–2019	256 (85)	646 (215)	183 (61)
2020–2025	199 (33)	799 (133)	170 (28)

Source: Fatalities 1988-2019, South Asian Terrorism Portal.

During the period 1989 to 2016, the SF suffered maximum casualties. The peak was in 2000 with 638 personnel making the supreme sacrifice. Annual average of SF casualties during the three year period from 1999 to 2001 was 594 personnel. Prior to this from 1996 to 1999 this average was 356. It was during this period that very large number of Kashmiri Pandits were persecuted and hence fled their ancestral homes in the valley. The figures shown in the table above do not include that number. Even the film 'Kashmir File' by Vivek Agnihotri on the atrocities committed on the Pandits created mixed reaction. Nevin Kallepali in Pulitzer Centre observes that the film (Kashmir Files) depicts the plight of Pandits in 1990 with stunning inaccuracies.....laden with scenes of violence so lurid it veers on parody'. In the beginning of his article he himself declares that the number of minority Hindus (Kashmiri Pandits) in the valley came down from 1,140000 in 1947 to just about 6500 now. This bewildering gap between observed facts and interpretation persists with a large segment in Indian population. Soldiers dying in any number and civilian casualties so far have been business as usual.

The Indian government took three major initiatives during these three distinct periods. First they crossed the Line of Control (LOC) in 2016 to get after the terrorists' camps. Three years later the Indian Air Force struck major terrorist camps across the International Borders. On 5 August 2019 the Articles 370 and 35 were abolished. All these actions have shown remarkable reduction in the loss of lives and terrorists' activities. In light of this the incident on 22 April 2025 was par with the trend. This time government of India wanted to lift the bar by several notches. That is where the 88 hours war with Pakistan fits in. As per the official statements by the political and military top brass from here on it is going to be – a long haul, whole of the nation era.

As regards India's response to the external threat we have seen the proactive actions India has taken in terms of self-reliance and political will to allow the armed forces a free hand.

REFERENCES

Data Sheet advanced Search Jammu and Kashmir https://www.satp.org/datasheet-terrorist-attack/fatalities/india-jammukashmir

Fatalities in Terrorists violence 1988-2019 https://www.satp.org/satporgtp/countries/india/states/jandk/data_sheets/annual_casualties.htm

https://www.dsci.in/resource/content/india-cyber-threat-report-2025

https://www.vifindia.org/article/2020/june/02/net-war-in-india-in-the-context-of-current-turbulence

https://www.indianretailer.com/article/retail-business/trends/67-pc-indians-turn-global-shopping-76-pc-trust-international-quality

https://www.deccanherald.com/opinion/it-s-the-quality-stupid-1185610.html

https://www.worldbank.org/en/news/press-release/2025/07/22/india-has-a-critical-opportunity-to-drive-resilient-urban-development-says-new-world-bank-report

https://www.translineindia.com/blog/smart-city-iot-solutions-internet-of-things/top-smart-cities-in-india-2025

Kallepalli Nevin (15 August 2024), 'To understand India Listen to the Pandits of Kashmir' https://pulitzercenter.org/stories/understand-india-listen-pandits-kashmir

THE FORCE BEHIND ECONOMIC GROWTH

BHARAT GLOBAL INDUSTRIES FORUM

LEADERSHIP TEAM

Chief Patron - BGIF, Chief Scientist, Zoho Corporation,

Awarded Padma Shri for his contribution to India's technological and economic landscape . Strong advocate for rural entrepreneurship self-reliance played key role in promoting decentralised innovation and skill development.

Dr. Amrit Sagar Mittal

Chairman - BGIF, Vice Chairman, Sonalika Tractor Group

Sonalika tractors is Globally recognised brand, the tractor is sold under the international brand name of Soli to more than 140 countries in the world. Sonalika is the third largest brand of tractors in India. Developed over 1000 tractor variants.

Mr. Rajkumar Goel

Vice Chairman: BGIF, Managing Director, SLR Metaliks

The SLR metaliks has successfully integrated alloy steel plant with renewable energy plant like solar, wind and hydro electrical production.

Mr. Yogesh Mehta

Secretary General - BGIF, Chairman, Vyankatesh Group

Export of extra low, low and medium and high ferro alloys including ferro magnese, ferro chrome ferro titanium and ferro molybdenum . Supplies high quality products to domestic and international markets.

Dr. Ashwin Johar

Founder Member: BGIF, Chairman, Sigma Group of Companies

Chairman regional economies since 2019 driven sustainable growth. Played key role in India Russia bilateral relations. Shaped India's economic discourse.

Mr. Pankaj Hans

Treasurer - BGIF, Managing Director, Competent Industries

Dynamic leader in construction and manufacture sectors. Emerged as one of the fastest growing manufacturers of construction equipment and heavy engineering fabrication services.

Dr. Raj Kumar

Founder Member: BGIF, Chairman, United Group of Companies

United group of companies overseeing business in food, textile, automotive and media. A top Indian flavour house advising FMCGs . Committed to advancing India's food sector.

Dr. Sidharath S. Sharma

Organisation Secretary: BGIF, Advisor, Cooperative, Government of Haryana

Specialist in strategic management, policy development and business growth. Alumnus of IIM Kozhikode . Played key role in employment generation revenue enhancement and operational efficiency across various domains. Currently serving as an adviser to Department of Cooperation Govt of Haryana.

The Bharat Global Industries Forum (BGIF) is a premier national platform committed to transforming Bharat into a **self-reliant, globally competitive industrial powerhouse**. Founded on the principles of **Swadeshi**, **sustainability**, and **innovation**, BGIF brings together the most influential voices in India's industrial ecosystem—including top corporations, policymakers, financial institutions, technocrats, and global investors.

BGIF was envisioned in alignment with the ideology of the **Swadeshi Jagran Manch**, which advocates for economic self-sufficiency and national industrial empowerment rooted in indigenous capabilities.

BGIF mission is to create a dynamic environment where **collaborative action**, **policy advocacy**, **international partnerships**, and **industrial innovation** converge to shape Bharat's future. Whether it's **driving large-scale manufacturing**, **fostering high-value exports**, or **catalyzing green and emerging technologies**, BGIF serves as a **catalyst for India's industrial renaissance**.

Through strategic forums, sector-specific engagements, whitepapers, and global outreach, BGIF is building a robust framework to unlock Bharat's potential as a global industrial leader by 2047.

Vision

To position Bharat as a world leader in industrial excellence by promoting innovation, fostering global investments, and unlocking international trade opportunities empowering Indian industries to drive sustainable economic growth and take centre stage in the global economy. We envision a future where India's industrial capabilities set global benchmarks for quality, resilience, and inclusivity. Through strategic collaboration and a strong national identity, BGIF aims to shape a self-reliant Bharat with global impact.

Mission

- **Promoting Indian Industries:** Showcase the strengths and opportunities of Indian industries, including manufacturing, technology, renewable energy, and emerging sectors, to attract global investors and partners.
- **Fostering Collaboration:** Build a dynamic networking platform that bridges Indian businesses with international stakeholders, facilitating mutually beneficial trade and investment opportunities.
- **Driving Innovation and Growth:** Encourage adoption of cutting-edge technologies and sustainable practices to enhance India's competitiveness in the global market.
- **Advocacy and Policy Engagement:** Partner with policymakers and industry leaders to shape policies that support industrial growth and streamline global collaboration.
- **Empowering Stakeholders:** Provide resources, insights, and connections to empower Indian companies in expanding their global footprint while enabling international businesses to seamlessly enter and operate in India.

Objectives

- To establish Bharat as a global manufacturing hub by promoting the potential of Indian industries, fostering international collaborations, and enabling sustainable growth across diverse sectors. Following are the
- To make India a ₹ 3000 trillion economy by 2047 (currently, it is approximately ₹ 350 trillion).
- To establish India as a global hub for manufacturing and exports.

- To provide quality employment opportunities to the youth workforce of India and the world.
- To make India a global centre for research and development.
- To position India as a focal point of global trust and respect.

* * *

Index